Integrated Spelling

GRADE 5

Harcourt Brace & Company

Orlando Atlanta Austin Boston San Francisco Chicago Dallas New York Toronto London

Printed in the United States of America

ISBN 0–15-307295-4

9 10 11 12 13   054   03 02 01 00

Contents

UNIT 4

UNIT 5

UNIT 6

Making Your Spelling Log

This book gives you a place to keep a word list of your own. It's called a **SPELLING LOG**!

If you need some **IDEAS** for creating your list, just look at what I usually do!

While I read, I look for words that I think are **INTERESTING**. I listen for **NEW WORDS** used by people on radio and television.

I will include words that I need to use when I **WRITE**, especially words that are hard for me to spell.

Before I put a word in my Spelling Log, I check the spelling. I look up the word in a **DICTIONARY** or a **THESAURUS**, or I ask for help.

To help me understand and remember the meaning of my word, I write a **DEFINITION**, a **SYNONYM**, or an **ANTONYM**. I also use my word in a sentence.

Here's how you use it!

THE SPELLING LOG SECTION of this book is just for you. It's your own list of words that you want to remember. Your Spelling Log has three parts. Here's how to use each part.

**SPELLING
★ WORDS ★**

Spelling Words to Study

This is where you'll list words from each lesson that you need to study. Include words you misspell on the Pretest and any other words you aren't sure you can always spell correctly.

This handy list makes it easy for me to study the words I need to learn!

I'll write a clue beside each word to help me remember it.

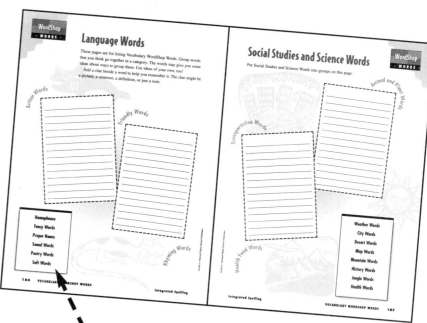

WordShop
★ WORDS ★

Vocabulary WordShop Words

These pages are for listing the WordShop Words from each lesson. Group the words any way you like, and write them on the pages where you think they belong. You'll find pages for language, social studies and science, and art and music.

Hints may help you think of categories for your words!

Your Own

My Own Word Collection

You choose the words to list on these pages. Include new words, interesting words, and any other words you want to remember. You decide how to group them, too!

Grade 5 • Harcourt Brace School Publishers

Study Steps to Learn a Word

Check out these steps.

1

SAY
THE WORD.
Remember when you have heard the word used. Think about what it means.

2

LOOK
AT THE WORD.
Find any prefixes, suffixes, or other word parts you know. Think of another word that is related in meaning and spelling. Try to picture the word in your mind.

Grade 5 • Harcourt Brace School Publishers

Integrated Spelling

SPELL
THE WORD TO YOURSELF.

Think about the way each sound is spelled. Notice any unusual spelling.

WRITE
THE WORD WHILE YOU ARE LOOKING AT IT.

Check the way you have formed your letters. If you have not written the word clearly or correctly, write it again.

CHECK
WHAT YOU HAVE LEARNED.

Cover the word and write it. If you have not spelled the word correctly, practice these steps until you can write it correctly every time.

SPELLING
★ WORDS ★

1. ask
2. says
3. shot
4. fact
5. does
6. gone
7. dance
8. health
9. loved
10. switch
11. watch
12. quit
13. busy
14. front
15. laughed
16. build

Your Own
★ W O R D S ★

Look for other words with short vowels to add to the lists. You might find *prince* or *realm* in a folktale.

17. _____
18. _____
19. _____
20. _____

Words with Short Vowels

Each Spelling Word has a short vowel sound: short *a* as in *add,* short *e* as in *end,* short *i* as in *it,* short *o* as in *odd,* or short *u* as in *up.* Look at the letters or letter pairs that have those same sounds. Sort the Spelling Words in a way that will help you remember them.

short a sound

short o sound

short i sound

short u sound

short e sound

▶ The short *a* sound can be spelled *a* or *au.*
▶ The short *e* sound can be spelled *ea* or *ay.*
▶ The short *i* sound can be spelled *i, u,* or *ui.*
▶ The short *o* sound can be spelled *o, a,* or *o–e.*
▶ The short *u* sound can be spelled *o, oe,* or *o–e.*

COAST TO COAST "Dear Mr. Henshaw" • Harcourt Brace School Publishers

Strategy Workshop

SPELLING CLUES: Visualizing When you want to learn to spell a word, look at it carefully. Then close your eyes and picture the word, concentrating on unusual letter groups.

Read the two columns of words. Visualize each correct spelling. Circle the misspelled words, and then write them correctly.

1. frunt   front   2. fack   fact
3. shot   shet   4. dance   danse
5. helth   health   6. build   bild

7–12. Proofread this notebook page. Circle the misspelled words. Then write them correctly.

> For my project I'm going to describe the day I rode with my dad, a truck driver. I'll tell how he turned on a swich to start the truck's motor, and how he shifted up and down through the gears. "How duz he do that?" I wonder, but I don't aske. I just wach him quietly, because he is so buzy driving and keeping his eyes on traffic. Dad sez he likes his work, and I believe him.

FUN WITH WORDS Write Spelling Words to complete what this boy is thinking about his father.

> That's my dad, who has **13** his truck since the day he bought it. The first time I saw the stripes along the sides, I **14**. I miss my dad because he is **15** so often, but I'm sure he'll never **16** his job.

1. _____
2. _____
3. _____
4. _____
5. _____
6. _____

7. _____
8. _____
9. _____
10. _____
11. _____
12. _____

13. _____
14. _____
15. _____
16. _____

Integrated Spelling

insulated
disconnect
triggered
fastened

SPELLING LOG Think about how you might use these words in your writing, and add them to your Spelling Log.

1. _____
2. _____
3. _____
4. _____

5. _____
6. _____
7. _____
8. _____
9. _____
10. _____

Vocabulary WordShop

Use the Invention Words to replace the numbers in this log. It is based on an idea in Beverly Cleary's "Dear Mr. Henshaw."

INVENTION #3: LUNCHBOX BURGLAR ALARM

I really needed a burglar alarm in my lunch box, so I bought some wire, a battery, a doorbell, and some tape. First I 1 one wire to the battery and another from the battery to the doorbell. Carefully I taped everything inside the 2 box. When I checked it later, the alarm was still 3 . At lunch, though, I had to open it, and then it went off! I was the only one who could 4 it!

5–10. What other words could you use in writing about an invention of your own? List them on the lines.

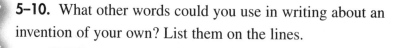

WHAT'S IN A WORD?

The word *truck*—including even a giant sixteen-wheeler—comes from the Latin word *trochus,* "iron hoop." Yes, the kind of hoop that kids used to roll down the street with a stick! Later, a *truck* was a revolving ring used in rifles. But what's the connection between a hoop and a truck? Well, the truck is named for the pin, or swivel, used to attach the trailer to the cab!

BEEP!

COAST TO COAST "Dear Mr. Henshaw" • Harcourt Brace School Publishers

Name _____

WORD HISTORIES Besides *truck,* the names of some other vehicles also have interesting origins. Write the name of the carriage that matches each item below.

1. The name of this carriage, known for its folding hood, is the word from which we get our word *cab.*
2. It was named for *Hackney,* a part of London in which people often rented carriages.
3. This one-horse carriage was named for the architect who designed it.

1. _____
2. _____
3. _____

SUFFIXES Suffixes are word endings that change either the meanings of words or the way the words are used. A farm, of course, is land used to grow crops. Add the suffix *-er* to *farm,* and you have *farmer,* the person who takes care of the farm.

The suffixes *-er* and *-or* mean "one who." If a *trucker* is one who drives a truck, who or what is:

4. a speaker?   5. a navigator?   6. a cleaner?

4. _____
5. _____
_____
6. _____
_____
_____

FLASHY PARTNERS Find a partner for this activity. Make five flash cards each, using the five short-vowel Spelling Words you find most difficult to spell. Exchange cards with your partner. Take turns asking each other to spell the words on the cards. Each time you've spelled a word, have your partner turn the card around so you can see whether you spelled it correctly.

COAST TO COAST "Dear Mr. Henshaw" • Harcourt Brace School Publishers

Words with Long Vowels

COAST TO COAST "Whose Side Are You On?" • Harcourt Brace School Publishers

SPELLING ★ WORDS ★

1. nine
2. cheese
3. plate
4. ray
5. chain
6. dream
7. cheeks
8. space
9. brain
10. slight
11. leave
12. tease
13. brief
14. style
15. straight
16. knight

Your Own WORDS

Look for other words with long vowels to add to the lists. You might find *dine* or *sweet* in a cookbook.

17. _____
18. _____
19. _____
20. _____

Each Spelling Word has a long vowel. You may remember that the long vowels "say their names," so the sound of long *a* is *a*, the sound of long *e* is *e*, and so on. Some combinations of letters also make long vowel sounds. Sort the Spelling Words in a way that will help you remember them.

long a sound

long e sound

long i sound

▶ The long *a* sound can be spelled *ay, ai, aigh,* or *a–e.*
▶ The long *e* sound can be spelled *ie, ea,* or *ee.*
▶ The long *i* sound can be spelled *igh, i–e,* or *y.*

Strategy Workshop

SPELLING CLUES: Guessing and Checking If
you're not sure how to spell a word, make a guess. Write it, and
then use the Spelling Dictionary to see if you're right.

Look at each pair of words. Guess which one is spelled correctly.
Then circle the misspelled word and write the correct spelling.

1. plat	plate	2. chane	chain
3. dream	dreme	4. knight	knite
5. stil	style	6. tease	teeze

7-12. Proofread this lost-and-found poster. Circle the six
misspellings, and then write the words correctly.

> Lost!
> Report card full of strat As, belonging to a real
> bran of a student! My cheks are red with shame
> for losing it, and I have only a reigh of hope that
> it will be found. Until I get it back, I am in slite
> trouble for being careless. Please lev phone
> number in Homeroom 3 if you can help!

FUN WITH WORDS Use the Spelling Words to
complete this person's feelings about living in the city.

I love living in the city. It's true that there's not much _13_, but it
does have advantages. I can make a _14_ visit to a museum and
then shop for the rest of the day. I can see _15_ new movies any
night of the week. And the place with the most delicious _16_
pizza in the world is open 24 hours a day! What more can I ask?

1. _____
2. _____
3. _____
4. _____
5. _____
6. _____

7. _____
8. _____
9. _____
10. _____
11. _____
12. _____

13. _____
14. _____
15. _____
16. _____

Integrated Spelling

Name _____

Vocabulary WordShop

Use the Math Words to replace the numbers in this paragraph.

Math
★ WORDS ★

angles
geometry
calculation
division

SPELLING LOG Exercise your mind! Think about using these Math Words in writing about topics not related to math. Add the words to your Spelling Log.

1. _____
2. _____
3. _____
4. _____

5. _____
6. _____
7. _____
8. _____

9. _____
   _____
   _____
   _____
   _____
   _____

MY SISTER—AMAZING, MATHEMATICAL AMANDA

Amanda has been a math whiz since she was four. I remember her peering over Mom's shoulder, asking questions as Mom did the household budget. Soon Amanda could do a <u>1</u> or two mentally. By the time she was seven, she knew long <u>2</u> and could figure some problems in her head. Lately, though, her new interest is the plane figures of <u>3</u>. Sometimes I'll come up behind her and watch her measuring with protractor and compass. "Well," I'll joke, "don't you know all the <u>4</u>!"

What words might you use to describe a friend or family member? Write them in a word web. Put the person's name in the center, and write the words around it.

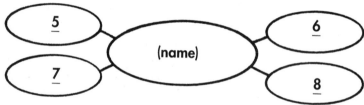

WHAT'S IN A WORD?

The English word *mathematics* came to us from Greek and Latin. Surprisingly, researchers have identified similar words in other early languages, showing that languages are linked together more closely than was thought.

One of the earliest words to which we can trace the word *mathematics* is the ancient Sanskrit word *medhā*, meaning "intelligence." Sanskrit was spoken by the East Indians thousands of years ago. The language of the barbarian Goths also had a related word, *mundon*, "to pay attention."

9. The early words *medhā* and *mundon* didn't mean "mathematics," but their meanings were related to the *idea* of math. How?

COAST TO COAST "Whose Side Are You On?" • Harcourt Brace School Publishers

Name _____

WORD HISTORIES Boston, Massachusetts, is named for a town in England. The English town was nearly called <u>Bo</u>tolph's <u>Stone</u>, but its citizens shortened its name to the underlined letters above.

Boston's nickname is *Beantown.* Why? Legend says that the settlers ate baked beans every Saturday night. Since their religion didn't allow them to work on Sunday (which began Saturday evening), they ate leftover beans that day instead of cooking!

Now think about a city you know well. Write its name on the line at the right. Add words to fit each heading below.

Name of City	1
famous places:	2
famous citizens:	3
nicknames:	4
famous sports teams:	5

1. _____
_____

2. _____
_____

3. _____
_____

4. _____
_____

5. _____
_____

CITY QUESTIONS Gather a small group, and play this version of Twenty Questions. One player chooses a Spelling Word that the others try to guess, using yes/no questions. (Does the word have any double letters? Does it contain a long *e* sound?) The student who uses the clues to guess and spell the correct word wins the round and becomes the next to choose a word.

Integrated Spelling

More Words with Long Vowels

COAST TO COAST "Shiloh" • Harcourt Brace School Publishers

SPELLING
★ WORDS ★

1. bold
2. true
3. rule
4. oak
5. soul
6. flute
7. owe
8. suit
9. lose
10. folks
11. clue
12. fruit
13. comb
14. throat
15. juice
16. prove

Your Own
★ WORDS ★

Try to find other words with long o and u sounds to add to your lists. You might find *drove* or *move* in a travel guide.

17. _____
18. _____
19. _____
20. _____

These Spelling Words have either a long *o* sound or a long *u* sound. Study the Spelling Words, and note the letter or letter pair that stands for each long *o* sound or long *u* sound. Sort the Spelling Words in a way that will help you remember them.

long o sound

long u sound

▶ The long *o* sound can be spelled *o, oa, ou,* or *o–e.*
▶ The long *u* sound can be spelled *o–e, ue, u–e,* or *ui.*

Integrated Spelling

Name _____

Strategy Workshop

SPELLING CLUES: Comparing Spellings If you don't know how to spell a word with a long *o* or long *u* sound, think about how the sounds are spelled. Choose the word that looks right to you.

Find the word in each group that looks right. Then circle the ones that look wrong. Write the word that is correct.

1. flote	flute	fluit	2. juce	juece	juice
3. throt	throut	throat	4. soul	soal	sowl
5. cloe	clue	cluoe	6. ruile	rule	ruel

7–12. Proofread this newspaper advertisement. Circle the misspelled words, and then write them correctly.

> **FOUND:** in owk grove in Friendly, male beagle, 2 years old; usual beagle color, but not bould; likes frute; might belong to fowlks who wanted to luse him; if owner can pruive ownership, I will buy pup for a moderate price; call 456-0773

FUN WITH WORDS Write Spelling Words to replace the numbers.

> Why am I out alone in this cold rain? I'm a good pup, yet my master mistreats me. If only I had a __13__ and gentle master, I would do anything to __14__ him. If he would take me inside, feed me, and __15__ my matted coat, I would __16__ him my life!

1. _____
2. _____
3. _____
4. _____
5. _____
6. _____

7. _____
8. _____
9. _____
10. _____
11. _____
12. _____

13. _____
14. _____
15. _____
16. _____

Animal Movement WORDS

slinking
barreling
loping
trailing

SPELLING LOG Can you use these words in a story of a happy day spent with a pet? Try it, and add them to your Spelling Log.

1. _____
2. _____
3. _____
4. _____

5. _____
6. _____
7. _____
8. _____
9. _____
10. _____

Vocabulary WordShop

Use the Animal Movement Words to replace the numbers in this cartoon.

At last Shiloh is mine! I love to see him __1__ along beside me or __2__ away into the high grass, looking for rabbits.

Here I am __3__ along at top speed! When I give my boy this stick, he'll praise me!

Good Shiloh! You'll keep __4__ along after me, I know, until I throw this again!

Write some other words that might describe how an animal feels and acts.

FEEL
5 _____
6 _____
7 _____

ACT
8 _____
9 _____
10 _____

WHAT'S IN A WORD?

Shiloh is the name of an ancient city in the Middle East. Long ago, people of many faiths considered it a holy place. So when they moved to other lands, they often called a new town *Shiloh* in remembrance.

In the United States there are many Shilohs, including one in Tennessee, the site of a great Civil War battle. A place near Friendly, West Virginia—the setting of Phyllis Reynolds Naylor's "Shiloh"—was called that too. How do we know? Because Marty named his pup for the place where he was found.

COAST TO COAST "Shiloh" • Harcourt Brace School Publishers

Name _____

WORD HISTORIES The endings of place names can often tell you what a place once was. Take *Lancaster,* a city in England. *Caster* comes from the Latin word *castra,* "camp." Many English cities whose names end in *-caster, -cester,* and *-chester* were sites of ancient Roman camps, where armies guarded the provinces. Now all that's left of the camps are a few ruins—and the great histories that their names recall.

Figure out the meaning of each town's name, below left, using the place-name endings and their meanings, below right. Then write the meaning of each town's name.

1. Sprucewold   a. *-bury* (mountain)
2. Millford   b. *-town* or *-ton* (town)
3. Lincolnshire   c. *-shire* (county)
4. Brookminster   d. *-minster* (monastery)
5. Southbury   e. *-ford* (river crossing)
6. Hillton   f. *-wold* (forest)

HOMOPHONES Homophones are words that sound alike but have different spellings and meanings. Match these homophones with their meanings. Write the correct meanings on the lines at the right.

7. clothes   in one side and out the other
8. close   shut
9. road   went for a ride
10. rode   propelled into the air
11. through   street, lane, avenue
12. threw   things to wear

RHYMING DOUBLES Work with a partner. Choose a Spelling Word, and see how many words each of you can write to rhyme with it. When you've done all you can, exchange papers. Try to add words to your partner's list, while he or she adds to yours. Choose different words and repeat the process.

1. _____
2. _____
   _____
3. _____
4. _____
   _____
5. _____
6. _____

7. _____
8. _____
9. _____
   _____
10. _____
11. _____
    _____
12. _____
    _____

SPELLING
★ WORDS ★

1. breeze
2. tuna
3. chili
4. tomato
5. coyote
6. tornado
7. potato
8. cargo
9. stampede
10. rodeo
11. patio
12. lasso
13. canoe
14. barbecue
15. vanilla
16. chocolate

Your Own WORDS

Look for other words that came to English by way of Spanish, and add them to the lists. You might see *mesa* or *arroyo* in a geography book.

17. _____
18. _____
19. _____
20. _____

Words from Spanish

Although many of these Spelling Words first came from Central or South American Indian languages, they entered English from Spanish. We have changed some of them a little, like *chili,* which in Spanish is *chile.* But many are spelled just like the originals—and have the same meanings as well. Sort the Spelling Words in a way that will help you remember them.

food words

western words

other words

► **Many English words come from Spanish.**

COAST TO COAST "Strider" and "Just My Luck" • Harcourt Brace School Publishers

Strategy Workshop

PROOFREADING: Comparing Spellings When you're proofreading, it's sometimes helpful to write a word in more than one way. Then compare the spellings, and choose the word that looks right to you.

Proofread these words across the columns. Look at each word, and decide which one is spelled correctly. Circle the misspelled words. Then write the correct spellings.

1. pateo	patio	poteo
2. tunar	touna	tuna
3. tomatoe	tomato	temato
4. lasso	lassoe	lassue
5. chili	chille	chily

1. _____
2. _____
3. _____
4. _____
5. _____

6–13. Proofread this diary entry made by a beginning runner. Circle the misspelled words. Write each word correctly.

> Today I did a few laps on the track for fun. What a shocker! I ran like a pototo rolling out of a grocery sack! I haven't been eating too much barbeqe or piling on the vanila and chocolete ice cream. But I'm terribly out of shape!
>
> Let's put it this way. If the track team runs like a tornadoe, I'm a poky breze. If I were in a rodao, I'd be stuck in a clown stampide. Monday I start some serious running!

6. _____
7. _____
8. _____
9. _____
10. _____
11. _____
12. _____
13. _____

FUN WITH WORDS Write Spelling Words to complete this cartoon.

C'mon, Juan! You're running like a truck with too much __14__. Imagine you're a __15__ chasing a rabbit!

Relax! Imagine you're a __16__ skimming across a lake!

14. _____
15. _____
16. _____

Integrated Spelling

Communication
★ WORDS ★

diary
journal
chatter
dialogue

SPELLING LOG How might you use the Communication Words in your writing? You may want to use them in a personal narrative or in a story about someone who keeps a journal. Add them to your Spelling Log.

1. _____
2. _____
3. _____
4. _____

5. _____
6. _____
7. _____
8. _____
9. _____
10. _____

Vocabulary WordShop

Use the Communication Words to complete these thoughts of a boy about his dog. In "Strider," Leigh wishes the dog could be all his, and not owned in "joint custody" with a friend.

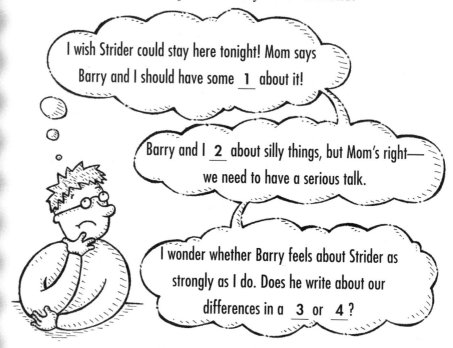

I wish Strider could stay here tonight! Mom says Barry and I should have some __1__ about it!

Barry and I __2__ about silly things, but Mom's right— we need to have a serious talk.

I wonder whether Barry feels about Strider as strongly as I do. Does he write about our differences in a __3__ or __4__?

Now think of some communication words of your own. Write them on the lines.

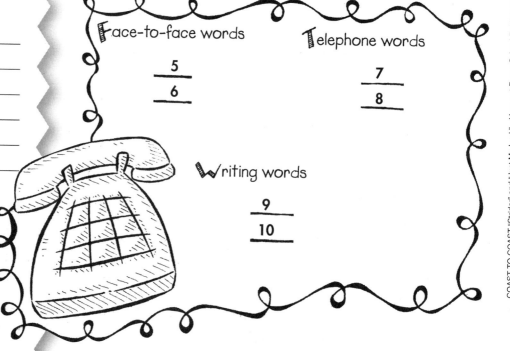

Face-to-face words

5 _____
6 _____

Telephone words

7 _____
8 _____

Writing words

9 _____
10 _____

COAST TO COAST "Strider" and "Just My Luck" • Harcourt Brace School Publishers

Name _____

WHAT'S IN A WORD?

Speaking of dogs, where do we get the expressions *dog days* and *dog in the manger*? The first one comes from ancient Rome. At that time, people thought that the hottest, most humid days of summer were caused by Sirius, the Dog Star. As a result, they called them *caniculares dies*—"dog days."

Dog in the manger comes from a Greek fable. In the fable, a dog sat by the hay in a manger, a box from which livestock eat. And even though the dog couldn't eat the hay himself, he wouldn't let the horses and cattle eat any either. Ever since, *a dog in the manger* refers to a person who keeps things from others even though he or she can't use them.

1. Give your own example of a person who is a "dog in the manger."

WORD HISTORIES Each word below comes from the Latin root *port,* meaning "to carry." Match each word with its definition. Write the letters of the correct answers.

2. porter	a. to carry goods into a country
3. import	b. to carry back news
4. export	c. capable of being carried
5. report	d. a person who carries things for others
6. portable	e. to carry from one place to another
7. transport	f. to carry goods out of a country

portable

NAME GAME Play this name game with a partner. Divide the Spelling Words so that you each have eight. Take turns giving clues for your words, such as rhymes, examples, "looks like" and "sounds like" clues, and synonyms or antonyms. Continue until all are guessed and spelled correctly.

1. _____
_____
_____
_____
_____
_____
_____
_____
_____

2. _____
_____

3. _____
_____

4. _____

5. _____
_____

6. _____

7. _____
_____

Practice Test

A. Read each phrase. On the answer sheet, mark the letter of the correctly spelled word.

Example: _____ my pet beagle

A lovd   B loved   C lovid   D lovde

1. has good _____
A helth   B heth
C health   D halth

2. _____ a lot
A lauht   B laughed
C laught   D lauft

3. _____ my father drive
A wach   B wacht
C wathc   D watch

4. the _____ that starts the engine
A switch   B swich
C swietch   D swetch

5. _____ very well in school
A does   B doz
C duz   D deos

6. _____ me too much
A teez   B teeze
C taez   D tease

7. made a _____ error
A slite   B slight
C sliet   D slyte

8. went _____ home
A strat   B straight
C strite   D strate

9. paddled in a _____
A canew   B canoo
C caneo   D canoe

10. ate a _____
A tomato   B tometo
C tomito   D tomatoe

EXAMPLE
A ⬤B C D

ANSWERS
1. A B C D
2. A B C D
3. A B C D
4. A B C D
5. A B C D
6. A B C D
7. A B C D
8. A B C D
9. A B C D
10. A B C D

Name _____

B. Read these word groups. Find the underlined word that is spelled wrong. On the answer sheet, mark the letter of that word.

Example: A an <u>oke</u> grove   B bowl of <u>chili</u>

   C good <u>folks</u>   D a <u>tuna</u> sandwich

1. A broke the <u>rule</u>   B likes <u>frute</u>
   C a <u>bold</u> speech   D <u>comb</u> my hair

2. A a <u>buzy</u> day   B the <u>front</u> door
   C one <u>shot</u>   D she was <u>gone</u>

3. A a cattle <u>stampede</u>   B a dance <u>step</u>
   C <u>build</u> a house   D <u>aske</u> directions

4. A lots of <u>space</u>   B a <u>breif</u> wait
   C <u>knight</u> in armor   D a <u>ray</u> of hope

5. A wash the <u>plate</u>   B one gold <u>chain</u>
   C rosy <u>cheks</u>   D a slice of <u>cheese</u>

6. A <u>nine</u> more days   B a happy <u>dreem</u>
   C <u>brain</u> waves   D <u>leave</u> early

7. A a sore <u>throte</u>   B lose my <u>voice</u>
   C orange <u>juice</u>   D a <u>true</u> statement

8. A <u>prove</u> my point   B a <u>clue</u> to follow
   C <u>quit</u> the job   D <u>sais</u> hello

9. A play the <u>flute</u>   B <u>owe</u> some money
   C a cool <u>breaze</u>   D heavy <u>cargo</u>

10. A <u>vanilla</u> ice cream   B <u>lasso</u> the calf
   C a hungry <u>coyot</u>   D <u>chocolate</u> milk

EXAMPLE

(A) (B) (C) (D)

ANSWERS

1. (A) (B) (C) (D)

2. (A) (B) (C) (D)

3. (A) (B) (C) (D)

4. (A) (B) (C) (D)

5. (A) (B) (C) (D)

6. (A) (B) (C) (D)

7. (A) (B) (C) (D)

8. (A) (B) (C) (D)

9. (A) (B) (C) (D)

10. (A) (B) (C) (D)

Unit 1: Writing Activities

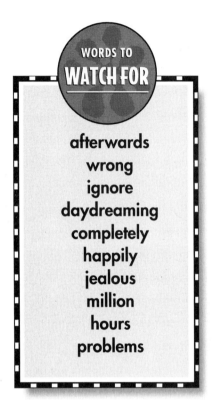

WORDS TO WATCH FOR

afterwards
wrong
ignore
daydreaming
completely
happily
jealous
million
hours
problems

So How Was the Weather?

Summer often brings severe and unexpected weather. Was your town or city visited by a hurricane? A long dry spell? A heat wave? Write an information paragraph about this summer's weather, using as many of the Words to Watch For as possible. Later, make a drawing to accompany your paragraph.

Tips for Spelling Success

- Make your best guess as you spell words you're not sure of.

- When you proofread, think about the letter combinations used in short-vowel and long-vowel sounds.

- Check previous lessons to be sure you've spelled everything right.

Read, but Don't Weep!

Tips for Spelling Success

Some of the funniest books have titles that don't sound funny at all. So check your library index under *Humor*, and read a few book summaries. Then jot down the most promising titles, double-checking the spelling of the author's name and the title of each book.

What are your personal goals for the school year? Do you plan to read an extra book or two on your own? If so, here's a suggestion: Read some humor! Humor can make you upbeat and confident. Even your health might improve! So *do* read a few funny books this year. Later, write a book report on one of them. Make your main idea the humor you enjoyed, and give examples from the book as details.

Name _____

It Can Happen Anytime!

Yes, the school year's for learning, but so is summer! In fact, the experts say that people learn best when they're not aware that they're learning! Did you improve your diving? Visit a new place? Make a new friend? Write a narrative telling what happened during the summer and what you learned. Use words that describe clearly the people or events that helped you. If you use a word that helps your reader picture someone or something exactly as you did, you've succeeded!

Tips for Spelling Success

When an adjective is made from a noun or a verb, the word's ending changes to show the new way the word is used. So the verb *change* becomes the adjective *change<u>able</u>*, and the noun *friend* becomes the adjective *friend<u>ly</u>*. Adjective endings you may want to watch for include *-ous, -y, -ful, -able* or *-ible, -less,* and *-some.*

Goodbye, Summer; Hello, Fall!

Now that the weather has changed, make "word trails" to lead from summer to fall. Think of one word that relates to summer and another that relates to fall. Use words with the same number of letters. Start by writing your summer word. Then make a trail of new words, changing only one letter at a time, until you reach your fall word. Here's an example:

warm · wart · cart · cast · cost · colt · coot · cool

Tips for Spelling Success

• As you work your way from one word to the next, think about the vowels you're using.

• Aim for the vowel sound in your target word.

• If necessary, review the letters that make that sound.

SPELLING
★ WORDS ★

1. round
2. spoil
3. town
4. noise
5. noun
6. frown
7. proud
8. boil
9. clouds
10. mouth
11. sound
12. drown
13. employee
14. shower
15. moist
16. employer

Your Own WORDS

Look for other words like *noise* and *town* to add to your lists. You might see *allowed* or *flower* on a garden sign.

17. _____
18. _____
19. _____
20. _____

Words Like *noise* and *town*

Words that include the *oi* and *ow* sounds need *digraphs,* or two-letter vowel combinations, to spell them. Study the digraphs that make those sounds.

Sort the Spelling Words in a way that will help you remember them. One example word is given. Fill in the other one as you are sorting.

coin

▶ The *oi* vowel sound can be spelled *oi* or *oy.*
▶ The *ow* vowel sound can be spelled *ou* or *ow.*

Integrated Spelling

COAST TO COAST "Morning Girl" • Harcourt Brace School Publishers

Strategy Workshop

SPELLING CLUES: Writing Aloud
When you are having trouble writing a word, try saying the word aloud. Listen to the sounds in the word, and think about the letters that usually spell those sounds. Then spell the word aloud as you write it.

Read these spelling pairs aloud. Circle the misspellings, and write the correct spellings.

1. toen   town
2. frown   frune
3. employer   emplouer
4. droan   drown
5. shower   shoyer

1. _____
2. _____
3. _____
4. _____
5. _____

6–9. Proofread this sailor's log. In the square, write the number of words he misspelled. Then write them correctly.

6. _____
7. _____
8. _____
9. _____

The sky was blue, and the sun was hot. Clouds swam in the sky and in the sea. Suddenly I saw a little girl in the water, swimming near our boat!
She opened her mowth, and I heard a sond but didn't understand her. I couldn't tell a non from a verb. Then she swam away.

FUN WITH WORDS
Use Spelling Words to complete the crossword puzzle. Write the answers on the lines.

10. _____
11. _____
12. _____
13. _____
14. _____
15. _____
16. _____

Name _____

Vocabulary WordShop

Use the People Words to complete the thoughts of Columbus and of the native child who swims out to meet his landing party.

My crew have been complaining and __1__ for months. They'll be glad to reach land at last!

How fat these visitors are! The fur on their faces makes them look __2__ !

I must be __3__ to them, since that is what my parents taught me.

What a __4__ child! The people here must be quite civilized!

5–8. Now think of four more words to describe people. Write them on the lines, and add them to your Spelling Log.

Lake	Seashore
5	7
6	8

WHAT'S IN A WORD?

What do you picture when you think of a canoe? A slim birchbark boat? Actually canoe comes from *canaoua*, a word for a large dugout boat used by the Arawak and Galibi peoples of the Caribbean.

People ★ WORDS ★

polite
courteous
grumbling
fierce

SPELLING LOG How can you use the People Words in your writing? Can they describe customers in a grocery store? Add them to your Spelling Log.

1. _____
2. _____
3. _____
4. _____

5. _____
6. _____
7. _____
8. _____

COAST TO COAST "Morning Girl" • Harcourt Brace School Publishers

Integrated Spelling

Name _____

PARTS OF SPEECH Many words can be more than one part of speech. For example, the noun *boat* means "a craft that floats." But the verb *boat* means "go out on the water in a boat." Read these pairs of sentences. Write each word and its part of speech.

Russell set the water on the stove to 1 .

Has the water come to a 2 yet?

Sad bugle notes 3 as the soldier is buried.

Don't make a 4 ; you may wake up the baby!

The weather report promises us a 5 today.

Raymundo will 6 before Sammi wakes up, so he'll have plenty of hot water.

1. _____

2. _____

3. _____

4. _____

5. _____

6. _____

WORD HISTORIES Words for various kinds of boats, ancient and modern, come from many languages. See if you can identify each boat shown, below.

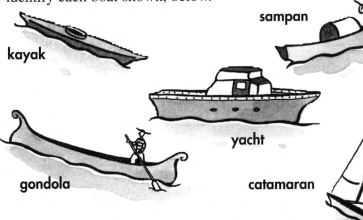

kayak

sampan

gondola

yacht

catamaran

7. Its name comes from the Inuit word *qajaq.*

8. Its name comes from the Dutch word *jaght*, short for the German *jachtschiff*, "hunting ship."

9. Its name comes from the Latin *gondula.*

10. Its name is a combination of *kattu*, "to tie," and *maram*, "tree."

11. Its name comes from the Chinese words *san*, "three," and *pan*, "plank."

7. _____

8. _____

9. _____

10. _____

11. _____

SELF-CHECK Choose the five Spelling Words that are the hardest for you. Write a sentence for each word, but leave a blank where the word goes. Put your paper aside for a while. Then go back to it and fill in the missing Spelling Words.

SPELLING
★ WORDS ★

1. bush
2. full
3. tall
4. cross
5. thought
6. cloth
7. brook
8. bought
9. taught
10. hood
11. wolf
12. caught
13. brought
14. offer
15. should
16. false

Your Own
★ WORDS ★

Look for other words with the vowel sounds heard in *fall* and *pull*. You might see *broth* and *cook* in a cookbook.

17. _____
18. _____
19. _____
20. _____

Words Like
brought **and** *full*

Each Spelling Word has the vowel sound heard in *brought* or the vowel sound heard in *full*. Think about the letters or letter combinations that spell these sounds.

Sort the Spelling Words in a way that will help you remember them. One example word is given. Fill in the other one as you are sorting.

cost

▶ The vowel sound in words like *brought* can be spelled *a, o, ough,* or *augh.*

▶ The vowel sound in words like *full* can be spelled *u, ou, o,* or *oo.*

COAST TO COAST "The Log of Christopher Columbus" • Harcourt Brace School Publishers

Strategy Workshop

PROOFREADING: Classifying Errors When you proofread, keep track of your spelling errors. Notice what kinds of mistakes you usually make, and work to correct them.

Proofread the words below. Circle the misspelled words. Use a caret (∧) to show where something is missing. Use a delete mark (⌒) to take out extra letters. Then write the words correctly.

1. caught	coaught	2. cros	cross	
3. bought	boht	4. falset	false	
5. wolf	wofe	6. tauht	taught	

7–11. Proofread these words that Columbus might have dictated to an assistant. In the diamond shape, record the number of errors his assistant made. Write the words correctly.

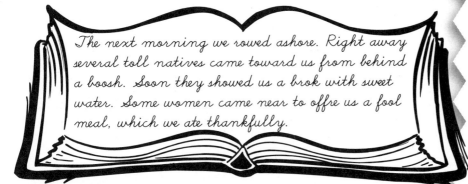

The next morning we rowed ashore. Right away several toll natives came toward us from behind a boosh. Soon they showed us a brok with sweet water. Some women came near to offre us a fool meal, which we ate thankfully.

1. _____
2. _____
3. _____
4. _____
5. _____
6. _____

7. _____
8. _____
9. _____
10. _____
11. _____

12. _____
13. _____
14. _____
15. _____
16. _____

FUN WITH WORDS Write Spelling Words to complete this cartoon.

Your Highnesses, I claimed the land for Spain and named it San Salvador. I __12__ you would be pleased.

Of course, you did as you __13__. But where are all the gold and silver you __14__ us?

Uh, Your Highnesses, the people had no gold or silver. But I do have some __15__. Won't it make a lovely __16__?

Integrated Spelling

Sea
★ WORDS ★

mast
embark
voyage
rigging

SPELLING LOG How can you use the Sea Words in your writing? For social studies class you could describe a fishing or whaling ship. Add the words to your Spelling Log.

1. _____
2. _____
3. _____
4. _____

5. _____
6. _____
7. _____
8. _____
9. _____
10. _____

Vocabulary WordShop

Use the Sea Words to complete the job offer sign. In "The Log of Christopher Columbus," Steve Lowe notes that Columbus had to offer extra wages just to find enough sailors for his ships.

SAILORS WANTED!

For historic _1_ to the Indies!

Applicants must know name and height of each

_2_ and must be able to climb into the _3_ at

any time, even during storms. Must swab decks.

If you can _4_ from Palos on 3 August, 1492,

see ship's officer inside. Good money for all!

5–10. What other words come to mind when you think of the sea? Write them on the lines at the left.

WHAT'S IN A WORD?

Can you imagine Columbus using pebbles to calculate distance? It may sound odd, but there's a connection between pebbles and calculating. It goes back to ancient Rome.

There, taxicabs were chariots. Before a trip, a box of pebbles *(calculi)* was set on the axle. As the wheels turned, the pebbles fell out—and the fare was "calculated" by the pebbles left in the box!

COAST TO COAST "The Log of Christopher Columbus" • Harcourt Brace School Publishers

Integrated Spelling

Name _____

CALCULATING WORDS
The Romans also invented words for special ways of calculating. The word *multiply,* for example, comes from the Latin words *multi,* "many" and *plicare,* "to fold"—as if in order to multiply, the person folded a number into layers!

Match the definition of each calculation with its name.

1. to take away   divide

2. to group into two or more parts   combine

3. to join in order to increase   subtract

4. to unite two items into one number   transform

5. to change one mathematical expression into another   add

1. _____
2. _____
3. _____
4. _____
5. _____

WORD DISCOVERIES
Each Spelling Word is hidden in the puzzle below. Work with a partner to outline all the Spelling Words and write them on the lines. For an extra challenge, work against the clock—or against another pair of classmates!

```
U G H T S H O U L D L Y O J K W O B R O U G H T U K S O S F I C I N G W A
F X F T F E R S O O S E F A U G H R C L E R O C E B T T K L X C T U R O T
C V E R A A O B U S H E F L R E R O I A A R Y B A H H T A E H R H O O L T
A T A L L C L O T H H H E S Y C R O S S U N U U G U G I E N U M F I R F E
C U L A I Z I S E S F C R T Y I K K E R I G U U U M G W E R G H U N O C E
P R A S L A R E E M I E B O U G H T I O M E A A A O C H T A H U L F F O T
R O S B L N O O H O O D R O P P I N G H O T T H O U G H T S S I L N I M R
```

6. _____
7. _____
8. _____
9. _____
10. _____
11. _____
12. _____
13. _____
14. _____
15. _____
16. _____
17. _____
18. _____
19. _____
20. _____
21. _____

COAST TO COAST "The Log of Christopher Columbus" • Harcourt Brace School Publishers

COAST TO COAST "Where Was Patrick Henry on the 29th of May?" • Harcourt Brace School Publishers

SPELLING
★ WORDS ★

1. smart
2. dirt
3. spare
4. order
5. forty
6. marched
7. pearl
8. shark
9. twirl
10. porch
11. circle
12. warn
13. earnings
14. quarter
15. declare
16. repair

Vowels Before r

The *r* in each of these Spelling Words gives the vowel or vowels that precede it a special sound. Study the patterns that spell these sounds.

Sort the Spelling Words in a way that will help you remember them. Three example words are given. Fill in the last one as you are sorting.

guard

stir

snort

Your Own
W O R D S

Look for other words with a vowel or vowels before r to add to your lists. You might see *earth* or *orator* in a social studies book.

17. _____
18. _____
19. _____
20. _____

▶ The vowel sound in words like *guard* can be spelled *ar*.
▶ The vowel sound in words like *snort* can be spelled *or* or *ar*.
▶ The vowel sound in words like *chair* can be spelled *are* or *air*.
▶ The vowel sound in words like *stir* can be spelled *ir* or *ear*.

Integrated Spelling

Strategy Workshop

PROOFREADING: Careful Pronunciation

When you proofread and are not sure of a spelling, say the word aloud. Think about the letters that usually make those sounds, and say each letter as you check the word.

Say each word below aloud. Circle the misspelled words, and write the ones that are correct.

1. porche   porch   pourch
2. order   arder   ordor
3. quater   quirter   quarter
4. repir   repair   repore
5. dirt   dort   dorte
6. porl   pearl   piarl
7. ornings   airnings   earnings

8–10. Proofread this practice speech. Read the words aloud. Circle the misspelled words, and then write them correctly.

> A man who helps King George is not a friend. Into our brave curcle of friends has mirched an enemy. Do not spaire him!

FUN WITH WORDS
Use the Spelling Words to complete these comments from some of Patrick Henry's listeners.

That Patrick Henry's a __11__ lawyer! And funny, too, I __12__ . Watch him __13__ that wig of his!

That man's a human __14__, and anyone who speaks against the colonies deserves to be bitten!

Ha ha! Somebody should __15__ King George!

It wouldn't help. One word from Mr. Henry, and __16__ regiments will be at his door!

1. _____
2. _____
3. _____
4. _____
5. _____
6. _____
7. _____
8. _____
9. _____
10. _____
11. _____
12. _____
13. _____
14. _____
15. _____
16. _____

Integrated Spelling

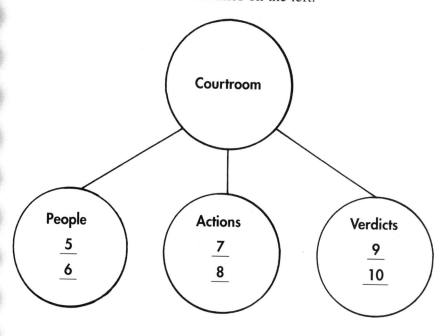

Courtroom
★ WORDS ★

opposition
lawsuit
petitions
retrial

SPELLING LOG Think about how you can use the Courtroom Words in your writing. Could you use them in a report? Add the words to your Spelling Log.

1. _____
2. _____
3. _____
4. _____

Vocabulary WordShop

Use the Courtroom Words to complete this court calendar. In "Where Was Patrick Henry on the 29th of May?" author Jean Fritz notes that Henry almost didn't take this famous case!

Court Calendar, Williamsburg, Virginia December, 1763

December 3 __1__ : Gray vs. State of Virginia
December 8 __2__ of Elijah Marshall, to purchase farmland from the county
December 15 remarks by Hon. Patrick Henry, in __3__ to the Parsons' Case
December 18 __4__ of George Witherspoon, upon finding of new evidence against him

5–10. What other words do you think of when someone mentions a courtroom? Write them on the lines on the left.

5. _____
6. _____
7. _____
8. _____
9. _____
10. _____

Courtroom

People
5
6

Actions
7
8

Verdicts
9
10

COAST TO COAST "Where Was Patrick Henry on the 29th of May?" • Harcourt Brace School Publishers

Integrated Spelling

Name _____

WHAT'S IN A WORD?

Lawyer is a word borrowed from Scandinavia. In Viking lands, each member of a group was bound to that group's customs and rules of life. The Vikings used the Old English word *licgan*, "to lay down," to mean those rules. That is, the rules were "laid down" as a base to build lives on. Later, *licgan* became *lagu*, "law," and those trained in law were known as lawyers.

WORD HISTORIES Legal terms often have surprising origins. *Sue*, for example, comes from the Greek word *hepesthai*, which means "to follow." (It reminds a lawyer to "follow up" on a case until it is settled.) To *plead* a court case comes from the Latin word *placere*, "to please." In fact, it's where we get the wording for the request "May it please the court."

DICTIONARY CHECK How's your "courtroom English"? Use a dictionary to find the meanings of these words. Write them on the lines.

1. _____

2. _____

3. _____

4. _____

The judge __1__ Patrick Henry's motion to give the parsons only a bit of what they demanded.

Later Patrick Henry requested a __2__ that prevented the parsons from having another hearing.

No matter how much the parsons grumbled, the judge __3__ every one of their lawyer's objections.

After his victory over the parsons, Patrick Henry won nearly every __4__ he argued in court.

COURTROOM DRAMA FACTORY Work with a partner to write a courtroom drama, using some of the Spelling Words. Try creating it on a computer, using clip art for illustrations. Afterward, share your drama with classmates.

plead

Integrated Spelling

COAST TO COAST "Dear Benjamin Banneker" • Harcourt Brace School Publishers

SPELLING
★ WORDS ★

1. _years_
2. _please_
3. _because_
4. _sure_
5. _ocean_
6. _clothes_
7. _sentence_
8. _practice_
9. _present_
10. _pressure_
11. _refuse_
12. _station_
13. _ancient_
14. _excited_
15. _machine_
16. _percent_

Your Own ★ WORDS ★

Look for other words that have the sounds /s/, /z/, and /sh/, and add them to the lists. You might see *cycles* or *observe* in a science book.

17. _____
18. _____
19. _____
20. _____

Words with /s/, /z/, and /sh/

These Spelling Words contain the sounds /s/, /z/, and /sh/. You may be surprised by the various letter combinations that spell these sounds.

Sort the Spelling Words in a way that will help you remember them.

seem

zero

sugar

▶ The sound /s/ can be spelled *c, s,* or *ce.*
▶ The sound /z/ can be spelled *s* or *se.*
▶ The sound /sh/ can be spelled *s, ti, ci, ce, ss,* or *ch.*

Name _____

Strategy Workshop

PROOFREADING: Reading Backward When you proofread, start with the last word and end with the first. Then read in the usual direction, slowly, for meaning.

Read these word groups from right to left. Circle the seven spelling errors. Then write the correct spellings.

1. thinks about the next sentance he will write
2. wonders about the close that plantation owners wear
3. will not refuze to answer my letter
4. pleas think of the wrongs done to slaves
5. a stacion in life much higher than mine
6. a slave cannot work like a mashine
7. so exited to receive Jefferson's letter

1. _____
2. _____
3. _____
4. _____
5. _____
6. _____
7. _____

Proofread the thoughts that Thomas Jefferson may have had. Read from right to left; then read from left to right. Circle the misspelled words. Then write them correctly.

8. Slavery is an ancent problem.

9. I hate it becase we are all created equal.

10. Yet in practize I can't run a plantation without slaves.

11. There is much pressaure to keep up traditions.

12. After many yearz I still struggle with my beliefs.

8. _____
9. _____
10. _____
11. _____
12. _____

FUN WITH WORDS Use Spelling Words to complete these almanac ideas. Write the words at the right.

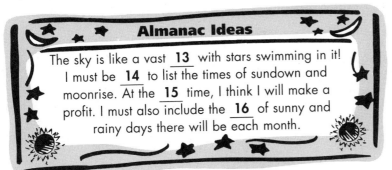

Almanac Ideas

The sky is like a vast __13__ with stars swimming in it! I must be __14__ to list the times of sundown and moonrise. At the __15__ time, I think I will make a profit. I must also include the __16__ of sunny and rainy days there will be each month.

13. _____
14. _____
15. _____
16. _____

Integrated Spelling

Name _____

Publishing
★ WORDS ★

publisher
manuscript
illustrator
editor

SPELLING LOG Think about using the Publishing Words in your writing. How would they be useful in news stories? Add them to your Spelling Log.

1. _____
2. _____
3. _____
4. _____

5. _____
6. _____
7. _____
8. _____
9. _____
10. _____

11. _____
12. _____
13. _____
14. _____

Vocabulary WordShop

Use the Publishing Words to tell how almanacs were once prepared and printed. In "Dear Benjamin Banneker," Andrea Davis Pinkney notes that Banneker's almanac almost didn't appear!

An __1__ reads the written words and makes corrections.

Type for the words in the __2__ is set by hand in a wooden page form using letters made of lead.

An __3__ draws pictures and maps for the almanac.

The almanac is printed, one page at a time. The __4__ is pleased.

5–10. Think of other words used in the field of publishing and write them on the lines at the left.

WHAT'S IN A WORD?

A *manuscript* is "written by hand." In Latin, *manu* means "by hand," and *scriptus* means "written." The new words below use some form of *manu* and *script*. Study the added word parts, and write the meanings of the new words. (Remember that word forms may vary from one word to another.)

New Word	Added Word Parts
11. inscribe	*in-* means "on"
12. manufacture	*facere* means "to make"
13. postscript	*post-* means "after"
14. manual	*-al* means "relating to"

Integrated Spelling

DICTIONARY DEFINITIONS   Information about an
entry word can help you spell, pronounce, and use the word
correctly. Study this entry. Then answer the questions.

The respelling shows how to say a word. The symbols between brackets [ ] represent sounds. The pronunciation key shows which symbol stands for which sound.

pub·lish [pub′lish] *v.* **1** To print and issue (as a book, magazine, or newspaper) for sale to the public. **2** To print and issue for sale the work of: We still *publish* Dickens. **3** To have one's work published: Our best-selling author *publishes* regularly. **4** To make known publicly: **Don't** *publish* your failures.

Each definition has a number. The most common one comes first.

Dots separate the entry word into syllables. The accent mark (′) shows which syllable is stressed.

Pronunciation Key

a	add	ô	order	zh	vision
ā	ace	oi	oil		
â(r)	care	ŏŏ	took	ə	**a** in about
ä	palm	ōō	pool		**e** in listen
e	end	ou	out		**i** in pencil
ē	equal	u	up		**o** in melon
i	it	û(r)	burn		**u** in circus
ī	ice	yōō	use		
o	odd	th	thin		
ō	open	th	this		

1. How many syllables does *publish* have?
2. Which syllable receives the stronger stress?
3. Is *publish* a noun, a verb, or a pronoun? How do you know?

1. _____

2. _____

3. _____

_____

_____

SYLLABLE-HAPPY   Challenge a partner to list the
Spelling Words in order by number of syllables. Begin with the
words with the fewest syllables and work up to those with the
most. But be careful! Lists must be numbered, and you can't
erase a word (or add one). The first person to make a correct
list wins.

Endings: -sure and -ture

SPELLING
★ WORDS ★

1. _adventure_
2. _capture_
3. _measure_
4. _feature_
5. _pasture_
6. _culture_
7. _structure_
8. _pleasure_
9. _treasure_
10. _mixture_
11. _lecture_
12. _creature_
13. _moisture_
14. _gesture_
15. _sculpture_
16. _furniture_

Your Own
★ W O R D S ★

Look for other words that end in -sure and -ture, and add them to the lists. You might see *closure* or *departure* in a mystery story.

17. _____
18. _____
19. _____
20. _____

These Spelling Words end in the suffixes -*sure* and -*ture*. Look at the letters that spell the sounds /zhər/ and /chər/. Then sort the Spelling Words in a way that will help you remember them. One example word is given. Add the other one as you are sorting.

posture
_____
_____
_____
_____
_____
_____
_____
_____
_____
_____

_____
_____
_____

► The /chər/ sound at the end of a word is spelled -*ture*.
► The /zhər/ sound at the end of a word is spelled -*sure*.

COAST TO COAST "A Gathering of Days" and "What's the Big Idea, Ben Franklin?" • Harcourt Brace School Publishers

Integrated Spelling

Name _____

Strategy Workshop

SPELLING CLUES: Ending Syllables

When you're not sure how to spell the last syllable of a word, pronounce the word carefully. Write the letters that usually make that combination of sounds.

Read these spellings across the columns. Then circle the misspellings, and write the words that are spelled correctly.

1. avensure	advenchure	adventure
2. pleasure	pleashur	pleature
3. jestsure	gesure	gesture
4. lecture	lecsure	lectur
5. feature	feetchur	featsure
6. creetur	creature	kreesure

1. _____
2. _____
3. _____
4. _____
5. _____
6. _____

Proofread this list of chores for a New England girl about your age. Circle the misspelled words. Write each word correctly.

7. Inspect henhouse walls for excess moischur.
8. Cook breakfast & add raisins to oatmeal mixsure.
9. Check on condition of new calf in paschure.
10. Bake bread; meture flour more carefully this time.
11. Make yogurt; use yogurt cultur sent by Mrs. Shipman.
12. Show Matty how to dust furnisure.

7. _____
8. _____
9. _____
10. _____
11. _____
12. _____

FUN WITH WORDS   Write the Spelling Word that matches each sketch below.

13.

14.

15.

16.

13. _____
14. _____
15. _____
16. _____

Name _____

Vocabulary WordShop

Use the Occupation Words to complete these advertisements.

Occupation
★ WORDS ★

carpenter
shoemaker
silversmith
blacksmith

SPELLING LOG How can you use these words? One possibility is in a social studies report. Add the words to your Spelling Log.

1. _____
2. _____
3. _____
4. _____

~WANTED~

__1__ to shoe horses and make metal tools; see Joshua Able at stables in Meredith.

LOOKING FOR STEADY WORK

__2__ makes boots and shoes for all ages; also harnesses and belts; contact Asa Reth in Meredith.

NOTICE TO ALL:

J. Whitlow, __3__, shall be in Meredith first week October. Fine silver utensils created to order. Make appointments with L. Butler, Meredith Feed & Grain.

NEEDED AT ONCE

__4__ to build baby furniture—cradle, crib, small chest. See new father, P. Allen, Meredith.

5. _____
6. _____
7. _____

8. _____

9. _____

5–8. What words come to mind when you think of occupations for today? Write them on the lines at the left.

WHAT'S IN A WORD?

To many, Ben Franklin is the father of electricity. But many centuries earlier, the Greeks had already learned that amber, which they called *elektron,* was magnetic.

Then, 25 centuries later, two English scientists made further discoveries. William Gilbert coined the word *electricus,* "electric." And Thomas Browne coined a term for what makes things magnetic. Yes, *electricity.*

9. List two forms of the noun *electricity.* Write each one's part of speech.

COAST TO COAST "A Gathering of Days" and "What's the Big Idea, Ben Franklin?" • Harcourt Brace School Publishers

48   **LESSON 10**

Integrated Spelling

Name _____

WORD HISTORIES Each word below comes from Greek.
Match these terms with their meanings. Write the letters of the
answers.

1. labyrinth   a. *komikos,* "to revel; to have a good time"   1. _____
2. poem   b. *osme,* "smell"   2. _____
3. odor   c. *labyrinthos,* "a maze"   3. _____
4. academy   d. *poiema,* "a composition in verse"   4. _____
5. comic   e. *marmaros,* "highly polished limestone"   5. _____
6. marble   f. *Akademeia,* "school in which   6. _____
                     Plato taught"

WHAT WAS THAT AGAIN? Play this word game
with a partner. Divide the Spelling Words evenly between you.
Then write your words in a list, but leave out all the vowels.
Draw a blank line next to each word. Then exchange lists with
your partner. Write each Spelling Word on the line next to the
consonant version. Here are two examples that use words other
than Spelling Words:

lctrc   electric   rrr   error

Which one of you guessed more words?

Integrated Spelling

Practice Test

A. Read each sentence. On the answer sheet, mark the answer that indicates whether the underlined word is spelled right or wrong.

Example: I heard a noise.

1. I'm so prowd of you!

2. You are ful of surprises today.

3. I thought you should take a rest.

4. Ashley marchd in the Thanksgiving Day parade.

5. I'm going to repare my bike.

6. Practis makes perfect.

7. Pleas excuse me.

8. The Pueblo have an advanced culture.

9. I think that answer is fals.

10. How long should I wait for you?

EXAMPLE	
● RIGHT	◯ WRONG

ANSWERS

1. ◯ RIGHT ◯ WRONG

2. ◯ RIGHT ◯ WRONG

3. ◯ RIGHT ◯ WRONG

4. ◯ RIGHT ◯ WRONG

5. ◯ RIGHT ◯ WRONG

6. ◯ RIGHT ◯ WRONG

7. ◯ RIGHT ◯ WRONG

8. ◯ RIGHT ◯ WRONG

9. ◯ RIGHT ◯ WRONG

10. ◯ RIGHT ◯ WRONG

COAST TO COAST Unit 2 Review • Harcourt Brace School Publishers

B. Read each sentence. On the answer sheet, mark the letter of the correct spelling.

Example: May I join your _____?

A curcle   B cercle   C circle   D curcl

EXAMPLE

(A) (B) ●C (D)

ANSWERS

1. Can you swim in the _____?
   A ocean   B oshen
   C oshun   D owcen

1. (A) (B) (C) (D)

2. It was a _____ meeting you.
   A pleasur   B plesure
   C plessure   D pleasure

2. (A) (B) (C) (D)

3. Please don't _____ my surprise.
   A spoyl   B spoil
   C spoile   D spoyle

3. (A) (B) (C) (D)

4. I want to take a _____ now.
   A shour   B showr
   C shower   D shor

4. (A) (B) (C) (D)

5. May I _____ you a snack?
   A offer   B offre
   C ofer   D offur

5. (A) (B) (C) (D)

6. We'll meet by the _____ at noon.
   A brouk   B brook
   C brok   D bruke

6. (A) (B) (C) (D)

7. What a wonderful _____ this is!
   A purch   B proch
   C porch   D pirch

7. (A) (B) (C) (D)

8. What kind of _____ is that?
   A structure   B strucktur
   C strokture   D structur

8. (A) (B) (C) (D)

9. Yes, that word is a _____.
   A nown   B knoun
   C noune   D noun

9. (A) (B) (C) (D)

10. This _____ ring was my grandmother's.
    A perl   B pearl
    C porle   D purle

10. (A) (B) (C) (D)

Unit 2: Writing Activities

WORDS TO WATCH FOR

thirsty
downstairs
whenever
chasing
tied
winning
slammed
jumped
proceed
sometime

"I'll Never Forget the Game When . . ."

What was the funniest or most spectacular thing you ever did while playing a game? Write a personal narrative telling what happened. First, give the time and place of the event. Then, picture the action and write it just as you visualized it. End the narrative by describing your own reaction or by telling what the crowd did. Use as many Words to Watch For as you can.

Tips for Spelling Success

• Remember that the effect of your narrative depends partly on what people said and shouted during the game.

• If you use slang expressions, spell them correctly and punctuate them as if they were ordinary speech.

Discovery!

Tips for Spelling Success

Check the spelling of the title and author's name before putting them on your display. Otherwise, someone who wants to read the book may be unable to find it.

What books have you read about discoveries? Draw a telescope on construction paper, cut it out, and paste it to a large cardboard sheet. For each "discovery" book you read, cut out a related object, such as a palm tree for the discovery of an island. Paste the object onto a small piece of construction paper, and write the book's title and author next to it. Arrange each "discovery" around the telescope. Give your display a title.

COAST TO COAST Unit 2 Review • Harcourt Brace School Publishers

This Is the Change We Want, and This Is Why

What? The computer lab isn't open after school? Write to the group that made the rule, and persuade them to change it. First, state clearly what you want. Next, list your reasons. Try to see the rule from the group's point of view. If they know you understand *their* reasons, they may be receptive to *yours*. To back up each reason, show how the change benefits everyone. Use strong, direct language.

Tips for Spelling Success

To find those forceful, persuasive words, use a thesaurus. Just be sure to choose words that are the same part of speech as the ones they replace! Look at the ending of the word you want to change. For example, if it ends in *-ive*, *-al*, *-ous*, or *-able*, choose an adjective. If it ends in *-ion*, *-ity*, or *-ence*, look for a noun.

Word Clues Today

Play a game of "Word Clues" with a partner. Choose a word. Make up two sentences that use the word in two different ways, but say *blank* in place of each word. For example:

The river enters the ocean at its *blank*. (*mouth*)
The child opened her *blank* but said nothing. (*mouth*)

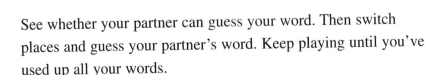

Tips for Spelling Success

Check the Spelling Dictionary for words that can be used as other parts of speech.

See whether your partner can guess your word. Then switch places and guess your partner's word. Keep playing until you've used up all your words.

COAST TO COAST Unit 2 Review • Harcourt Brace School Publishers

SPELLING
★ WORDS ★

1. played
2. lived
3. teaching
4. pleased
5. amazing
6. changed
7. walking
8. named
9. turned
10. watched
11. cried
12. writing
13. supposed
14. practicing
15. surprised
16. becoming

Your Own WORDS

Look for other words that end with *-ed* and *-ing*, and add them to the lists. *Dancing* or *rippling* can describe the surface of a lake.

17. _____
18. _____
19. _____
20. _____

Endings: -ed and -ing

All the Spelling Words end with *-ed* or *-ing*. As you spell each word, notice any changes made to the base word when the ending is added.

Sort the Spelling Words in a way that will help you remember them. You may want to list them by the way you add the endings to the base words.

danced

spied

harmed

▶ For base words ending with *e*, drop the *e* before adding *-ed* or *-ing*.
▶ For base words ending with *y* preceded by a consonant, change the *y* to *i* before adding *-ed*.
▶ For most other base words, simply add the ending.

Integrated Spelling

Strategy Workshop

PROOFREADING: Working Together When you proofread, work with a partner. Read the words aloud as your partner looks at the spellings. Then trade jobs.

Read across the columns. Which words just don't look right? Work with a partner to find and circle the six misspellings. Take turns circling words and writing them correctly.

1. changed   changd   2. practiceing   practicing
3. writeing   writing   4. plaed   played
5. teaching   teacheing   6. watched   wached

Proofread these comments that might have been made by a ten-year-old coming to the United States for the first time. Take turns circling misspellings and writing them correctly.

7. At the Golden Gate I cryed, "This is my country!"
8. Are these cars supposd to go so fast?
9. The hills have turnd into such beautiful countryside!
10. What an amazeing plant a cactus is!
11. I've namd some of these lovely flowers myself.
12. Grandmother was surprisied to see how tall I am.

FUN WITH WORDS Use Spelling Words to complete this diary entry. Write the best word on each line.

August 24

I'm so __13__ to be here with Grandmother. Each day we go __14__, and I tell her how we __15__ in China. But that was long ago, and each day I am __16__ more American.

1. _____
2. _____
3. _____
4. _____
5. _____
6. _____

7. _____
8. _____
9. _____
10. _____
11. _____
12. _____

13. _____
14. _____
15. _____
16. _____

Ocean Liner
★ WORDS ★

shipboard
bunk
smokestack
deck

SPELLING LOG Think about using the Ocean Liner Words in your writing. They might be useful in a group called *Adventure Words*. Add them to your Spelling Log.

1. _____
2. _____
3. _____
4. _____

5. _____
6. _____
7. _____
8. _____
9. _____
10. _____

11. _____
12. _____

_____

Vocabulary WordShop

Use an Ocean Liner Word to complete each imaginary headline.

FRITZ ON __1__ —RETURNING TO STATES NEXT WEEK!
FRITZ COLLIDES WITH SHIP'S __2__ IN RACE WITH FRIEND
FRITZ CONFINED TO __3__ AFTER RACE INJURY
FRITZ FINALLY ON __4__ FOR FIRST GLIMPSE OF USA!

What other words come to mind when you think of ocean liners? Write them on the lines at the left.

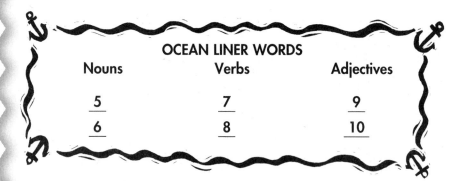

OCEAN LINER WORDS

Nouns	Verbs	Adjectives
5	7	9
6	8	10

WHAT'S IN A WORD?

Why is the right side of a ship *starboard* and the left *larboard*? *Starboard* comes from the Old English word *steor-bord*, "steering side," because in Viking ships, the steering oar was on the right. *Larboard* comes from *lade-bord*, which means "loading side." With the steering oar on the right, the ship had to be loaded from the left. *Port* is a later word for *larboard*. It came about because the loading side was always brought alongside the port's docks.

11. According to the paragraph, what did the word *bord* mean?

12. Make up a silly sentence or other mnemonic device to help you remember that the left side of a ship is the port side.

COAST TO COAST "Homesick: My Own Story" • Harcourt Brace School Publishers

GREAT VERBS   Newspaper headlines are meant to catch the reader's eye. That's why they're printed in such large letters —and also why the verbs are so precise.

To write great verbs of your own, close your eyes and visualize the action. Use the sharpest, most precise verb you can think of. But don't stop there. Check a thesaurus, or dictionary of synonyms, to find the most accurate verb of all.

The three words after each question below might be listed together in a thesaurus. Choose the most precise word and write it on the answer line.

1. **Which verb best describes the movement of a small, swift boat?**
   a. sailed   b. scudded   c. hovered
2. **Which verb best describes the motion of a badly overloaded boat?**
   a. careening   b. reeling   c. staggering
3. **Which verb best describes the movement of a swift warship?**
   a. flitted   b. scooted   c. sped

1. _____

2. _____

3. _____

WORD HISTORIES   What word names a group of ships? *Fleet* comes from the Old English word *fleot,* "ship." Long ago, a *fleet* was a group of warships. Today it includes trading ships and other carriers under a single command. *Armada* and *flotilla* are Spanish words that also once meant a group of warships. Now they mean any large group of moving things, even trucks!

Argosy comes from the Italian word *Ragusea,* "a ship from Ragusa, Sicily." Later, *argosy* named any large merchant ship— and even a fleet/armada/flotilla/argosy of them!

ROUND-ROBIN   In a group with two or three classmates, write a round-robin story about a new student who has lived for a long time in another country. As the paper is passed around, each person adds a sentence using one of the Spelling Words. Keep going until all the Spelling Words have been used.

SPELLING ★ WORDS ★

1. covered
2. opening
3. visiting
4. ordered
5. entered
6. forgetting
7. regretted
8. suffered
9. happened
10. gathering
11. permitted
12. referred
13. controlled
14. wondering
15. remembered
16. flustered

Your Own ★ WORDS ★

Try to find other words that end in *-ed* and *-ing*. *Answered* or *compelling* might be in a magazine article.

17. _____
18. _____
19. _____
20. _____

Endings: More
-ed and *-ing*

Like the words in Lesson 12, these Spelling Words end in *-ed* and *-ing*. As you read the list, notice how each ending is added.

Sort the Spelling Words in a way that will help you remember them. One example word is given. Fill in the other one as you are sorting.

sharpened

▶ Just add *-ed* or *-ing* to words with an unstressed final syllable.

▶ Double the final consonant before adding *-ed* or *-ing* to words accented on the last syllable.

COAST TO COAST "Mary McLeod Bethune, Dream Maker" • Harcourt Brace School Publishers

Integrated Spelling

Strategy Workshop

SPELLING CLUES: Visualizing When you are learning a word, look at it carefully. Then close your eyes and picture it, concentrating on unusual letter groups.

Read the words below. Visualize each correct spelling. Circle the incorrect word in each group, and then write the word correctly at the right.

1. flustered   flusterd   2. coverd   covered
3. forgeting   forgetting   4. hapened   happened
5. visitting   visiting

6–11. Proofread the news story below. Circle the misspelled words. Then write the words correctly.

MARY MCLEOD BETHUNE CELEBRATES COLLEGE'S 50TH ANNIVERSARY

"Today I remembered when only five students had enterred these walls," said Mrs. Bethune, president of Bethune-Cookman College. "We sufferd a lot back then. Openning a college for black students was difficult, but I haven't regreted a thing."

Today, as students were gatherring for graduation, Mrs. Bethune also thought about the future.

FUN WITH WORDS Use Spelling Words to complete the crossword puzzle. Write the words at the right.

1. _____
2. _____
3. _____
4. _____
5. _____

6. _____
7. _____
8. _____
9. _____
10. _____
11. _____

12. _____
13. _____
14. _____
15. _____
16. _____

Vocabulary WordShop

reminiscing
resigned
evasively
solemnly

SPELLING LOG Think about how you might use the Speech Words in your writing. They seem natural for a short biography. Add the words to your Spelling Log.

1. _____

2. _____

3. _____

4. _____

In "Mary McLeod Bethune, Dream Maker," Mrs. Bethune thinks about her youth. Use the Speech Words to complete sentences about her first days of teaching.

 In our first school I had to answer the building inspectors __1__ . Some of the work had not yet been completed!

 I was __2__ about the time Booker T. Washington visited us. We had only one small, wooden building to show him.

 I was __3__ to having a wooden school, but things soon improved. We even built a college of stone.

 Today I __4__ promise that I will not stop teaching as long as I am needed!

5-8. Now think of other words you can use to write about people and their messages. Write them on the lines at the left.

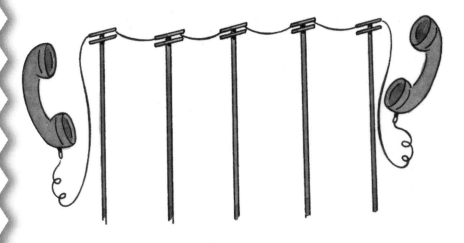

5. _____

6. _____

7. _____

8. _____

COAST TO COAST • "Mary McLeod Bethune, Dream Maker" • Harcourt Brace School Publishers

Integrated Spelling

Name _____

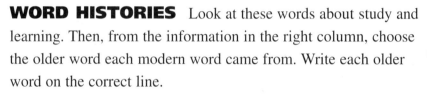

*C*ollege comes from the Latin word *collegium,* "society." During the Middle Ages a *college* was a group of priests. They lived and studied together, supported by the local political leader. At that time, priests were among the few to receive an education.

Today *college* has two general meanings. First, it can be part of a university, a large school with many divisions. Each *college* of the university offers courses in certain fields of study. A *college* may also be an independent school that offers courses in general fields.

WORD HISTORIES Look at these words about study and learning. Then, from the information in the right column, choose the older word each modern word came from. Write each older word on the correct line.

1. teacher	Old English *leornian*	1. _____
2. student	Old English *writan,* "to scratch, draw"	2. _____
3. read	Latin *gradus,* "step"	3. _____
4. learn	Latin *rememorari,* "to be mindful of again"	4. _____
5. school	Latin *studens,* "eager for learning"	5. _____
6. remember	Old English *taecan,* "to show"	6. _____
7. examination	Middle English *reden,* "to advise, interpret"	7. _____
8. spell	Greek *schole,* "discussion"	8. _____
9. graduate	Latin *examen,* "inspect closely"	9. _____
10. write	Greek *apeilē,* "boast"	10. _____

SELF-CHECK Choose seven Spelling Words whose spellings you are trying to learn. Write a sentence for each word, but leave a blank where the word goes. Put your paper aside for a while. Go back to it later, and fill in the Spelling Words. Check your spelling!

Unstressed Endings: /ən/ and /ər/

1. dragon
2. button
3. tower
4. human
5. dozen
6. frozen
7. flavor
8. chapter
9. oven
10. factor
11. canyon
12. rather
13. terror
14. daughter
15. woman
16. odor

Each Spelling Word is a two-syllable word that ends with *n* or *r* preceded by *a*, *e*, or *o*. The second syllable of each word is not accented. It has a weak vowel sound called a schwa (ə).

Sort the Spelling Words in a way that will help you remember them. Two example words are given.

apron
_____
_____
_____
_____
_____
_____
_____

banner
_____
_____
_____
_____
_____
_____
_____

Look for other words with /ən/ and /ər/, and add them to the lists. *Dinner* and *dollar* might be on an airline poster.

17. _____
18. _____
19. _____
20. _____

▶ The unstressed sound /ər/ can be spelled *er* or *or*.
▶ The unstressed sound /ən/ can be spelled *an*, *en*, or *on*.

COAST TO COAST "Nickel-a-Pound Plane Ride" • Harcourt Brace School Publishers

Integrated Spelling

Strategy Workshop

SPELLING CLUES: Writing Aloud When you are learning to spell a word, it is sometimes helpful to say each letter aloud as you practice writing the word.

Circle each misspelling. Then, as you write the words correctly on the lines, say each letter to yourself.

1. human   humen   2. butten   button

3. oder   odor   4. ovan   oven

5. frozen   frozan   6. chaptar   chapter

7–11. Proofread this newspaper ad. Circle the misspellings. Write the words correctly on the lines.

PLANE RIDES FOR A NICKEL A POUND TO BENEFIT CHILDREN'S HOSPITAL

Always wanted to fly? Rathor keep it short?
DRAGEN AIRWAYS, sponsor of sightseeing flights,
welcomes you! The price is great—and when you facter
in a gift to charity, you have an unbeatable deal!
Bring your son! Bring your daughtor!

FLY OVER KEARNY PARK!
SEE THE FRESNO WATER TOWAR!

FUN WITH WORDS Use the Spelling Words to complete the newswoman's interview with two first-time fliers.

12 :

How was the ride? Did it help you capture the 13 of Fresno?

Are you kidding? The ride was a 14 from start to finish! I was sure I'd fall into a 15 and never be heard from again!

But I *loved* it! I'd take a 16 more rides if I could!

1. _____

2. _____

3. _____

4. _____

5. _____

6. _____

7. _____

8. _____

9. _____

10. _____

11. _____

12. _____

13. _____

14. _____

15. _____

16. _____

Integrated Spelling

Demeanor ★ WORDS ★

baffled
determined
earnest
perplexed

SPELLING LOG Think about how you can use the Demeanor Words in your writing. You may want to add them to your Spelling Log in one of your describing categories.

1. _____
2. _____
3. _____
4. _____

Vocabulary WordShop

In "Nickel-a-Pound Plane Ride," Araceli's reaction to her first flight is completely unexpected. Use the Demeanor Words to complete her explanation.

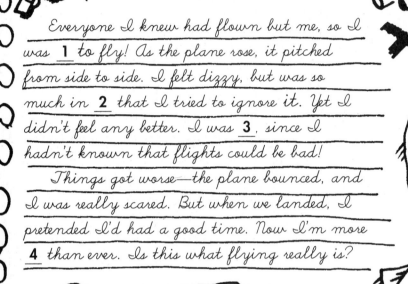

Everyone I knew had flown but me, so I was __1__ to fly! As the plane rose, it pitched from side to side. I felt dizzy, but was so much in __2__ that I tried to ignore it. Yet I didn't feel any better. I was __3__, since I hadn't known that flights could be bad!

Things got worse—the plane bounced, and I was really scared. But when we landed, I pretended I'd had a good time. Now I'm more __4__ than ever. Is this what flying really is?

5-10. Think of other words that show how people feel, what they say, and how they act. Write them on the lines.

Feel	Say	Act
5	7	9
6	8	10

5. _____
6. _____
7. _____
8. _____
9. _____
10. _____

WHAT'S IN A WORD?

Americans were proud of Charles Lindbergh when, in 1927, he became the first pilot to fly alone across the Atlantic. As a result, many things were named for him, one of the oddest being the Lindy Hop.

The Lindy Hop is a dance invented in Harlem, New York. You can see that *Lindy* is short for *Lindbergh,* but how are a dance and a flier related? Back then, *hop* was slang for two things: a dance party and a short airplane flight!

Integrated Spelling

Name _____

WORD HISTORIES What's the difference between a puddle-jumper and a jumbo jet? A puddle-jumper is a small plane used for short trips. A jumbo jet is a large plane that flies long distances. But why call it *jumbo*?

The *Jumbo* that gave many things their names was an elephant in P.T. Barnum's circus. He was 10 feet 9 inches tall at the shoulder and weighed 6 1/2 tons. Yet, when he was killed by a freight train in 1885, a bone study showed that he was not even fully grown! Now *that's* jumbo!

Match these "flying" items with the definitions and origins of their names. Write the letters of the correct answers on the lines.

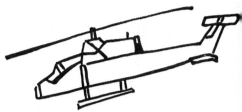

1. _____
2. _____
3. _____
4. _____
5. _____

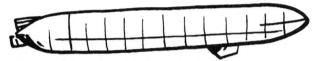

1. turboprop
2. diesel
3. blimp
4. zeppelin
5. helicopter

a. engine used in planes; named for its inventor, Rudolf Diesel

b. observation balloon named for Colonel Blimp, a cartoon character

c. airship powered by rotors; from Greek *heliko,* "stem," and *pteron,* "wing"

d. airplane engine with propellers (props) as well as a jet engine (turbo)

e. airship named for a German count, Ferdinand von Zeppelin

HAPPY ENDINGS Play this game with two classmates. Two players each hold cards with the Spelling Word endings *an, en, on, er,* and *or* on them. The third player faces them and calls out a Spelling Word. The first two hold up cards with the endings they think are correct. Each correct ending earns one point. The player with the greater number of points at the end of the game wins.

COAST TO COAST • "The Nickel-a-Pound Plane Ride" • Harcourt Brace School Publishers

Integrated Spelling

Unstressed Endings: /əl/

1. simple
2. battle
3. evil
4. metal
5. level
6. formal
7. cattle
8. single
9. animal
10. double
11. model
12. civil
13. couple
14. council
15. trial
16. needle

Your Own ★ WORDS ★

Look for other words that end with /əl/ and add them to the lists. You might see *signal* and *channel* in a TV magazine.

17. _____
18. _____
19. _____
20. _____

Each Spelling Word ends with the sounds /əl/. Study the letter combinations that spell these sounds.

Sort the Spelling Words in a way that will help you remember them. Three example words are given. Add the fourth one as you are sorting.

barrel

pencil

sample

▶ The unstressed ending /əl/ can be spelled *el, le, al,* or *il.*

Integrated Spelling

Strategy Workshop

SPELLING CLUES: Syllable Patterns When you are learning to spell a two-syllable word, study the pattern of letters in each syllable. Look for similar patterns in other words.

The missing syllable of each Spelling Word is pronounced /əl/. Think of the missing letters. Then write each Spelling Word.

1. catt____ in the field
2. doub____ dip
3. no form____ training
4. a civ____ matter
5. need____ in a haystack
6. the city counc ____

7–13. Proofread the list of skills in this description of a survival course. Circle the misspelled words. Then write them correctly on the lines.

> **SURVIVAL TRAINING COURSE, BASIC SKILLS LEVAL**
> Simpal forest survival methods
> Mountain skills (singel person)
> Mountain skills (coupil or group)
> Use of survival kit (modal A or B)
> ALSO
> Animel behavior in the wild
> Special uses for common metel objects

WORKING WITH MEANING Use Spelling Words to replace 14-16. A plane-crash survivor began this journal.

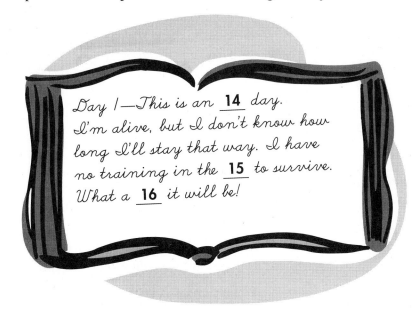

Day 1—This is an __14__ day. I'm alive, but I don't know how long I'll stay that way. I have no training in the __15__ to survive. What a __16__ it will be!

1. _____
2. _____
3. _____
4. _____
5. _____
6. _____

7. _____
8. _____
9. _____
10. _____
11. _____
12. _____
13. _____

14. _____
15. _____
16. _____

Name _____

Vocabulary WordShop

Use Airplane Words to complete this airplane manual page.

Airplane
★ **WORDS** ★

altimeter
airspeed
dashboard
fuselage

SPELLING LOG Think about using Airplane Words in your writing. You might put them in a list of words for adventures. Add them to your Spelling Log.

1. _____
2. _____
3. _____
4. _____

5. _____
6. _____
7. _____
8. _____
9. _____
10. _____
11. _____
12. _____

13. _____
_____
_____
_____
_____
_____
_____
_____

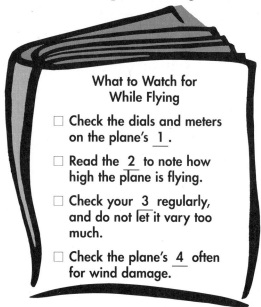

What to Watch for While Flying

☐ Check the dials and meters on the plane's __1__.

☐ Read the __2__ to note how high the plane is flying.

☐ Check your __3__ regularly, and do not let it vary too much.

☐ Check the plane's __4__ often for wind damage.

5–12. What other words come to mind when you think of airplanes? Write them under these headings.

Flight Words
5   6

Destinations
7   8

Airplane Words

Airplane Parts
9   10

Airplane Careers
11   12

WHAT'S IN A WORD?

You probably think of a hatchet as a tool for chopping down trees, but long ago it was used for other things. The ancient German hatchet was the *happa*, a sickle used to harvest grain. The early French had the *hache*, a long-handled battle ax. Later, English woodworkers shortened the handle, gave it the name *hatchet*, and used it to cut wood.

13. What do the words *happa, hache,* and *hatchet* all tell you about the way the English language grew? Write your answer on the lines.

Name _____

WORD HISTORIES   The tools used for survival have not
changed much over the years. And even if the origins of their
names are different, the tools themselves are known the world
over. Match the names of these tools with the words from which
they came. Write each correct source word.

1. knife	Old German *flins,* "pebble"	1. _____
2. rope	Old French *compasser,* "to measure"	2. _____
3. flint	Old German *reif,* "hoop"	3. _____
4. fishhook	Old English *hoc*	4. _____
5. compass	Old English *cnif*	5. _____

SIMILES   Similes are comparisons of two unlike things,
using *like* or *as*. Similes make writing more descriptive. Read
these similes. Then write the answers to the questions.

**Trudging through deep snow is like wading through white mud.
The hatchet cut through ice as a warm knife cuts through butter.**

6. What two things are compared in the first simile?
7. What is the writer saying about these two things?
8. What two things are compared in the second simile?
9. What idea is the writer communicating about them?

6. _____
_____
7. _____
_____
_____
8. _____
_____
9. _____
_____
_____
_____

SPELLING PASSWORD   Choose a partner for this
game. Write the Spelling Words from this lesson on slips of
paper. Put the folded slips in a box. One player draws a slip and
begins the game by giving a clue for the word on the slip. One
clue might be "A raccoon is an _____." Take turns giving clues
and guessing and spelling the words.

Name _____

Troublesome Words and Phrases

SPELLING ★ WORDS ★

1. there's
2. everyone
3. theirs
4. every one
5. all ready
6. who's
7. a lot
8. every day
9. whose
10. all right
11. everyday
12. already
13. altogether
14. all together
15. any way
16. anyway

Your Own WORDS

List some other troublesome words and phrases. You might find *sometime* and *some time* in a dialogue.

17. _____
18. _____
19. _____
20. _____

These Spelling Words are among the most frequently misspelled words in the English language. They include contractions; individual words or compound words that are written as one word; and two-word phrases. Within the list you will notice several pairs of homophones that are easily mistaken for each other.

Sort the Spelling Words in a way that will help you remember them.

written as one word

written as a contraction

written as two words

▶ Words and phrases that sound similar to one another will not be as troublesome if you remember which spelling goes with which usage.

COAST TO COAST "Pride of Puerto Rico:Roberto Clemente" and "In the Year of the Boar and Jackie Robinson" • Harcourt Brace School Publishers

Name _____

Strategy Workshop

SPELLING CLUES: Thinking About Meaning

When you use a word or phrase that has a homophone, learn the meanings of both words. Think about the meanings as you write.

Think about the meaning of each sentence. Underline the correct homophone in parentheses and then write it.

1. I'm not (altogether, all together) happy with my work.
2. Staple the pages (altogether, all together) into a book.
3. These are my (everyday, every day) shoes.
4. (Everyday, Every day) that I'm here, I feel more welcome.
5. (Who's, Whose) there?
6. (Who's, Whose) pen is this?

1. _____
2. _____
3. _____
4. _____
5. _____
6. _____

7–12. Proofread this child's letter to her family in China. Circle the misspellings. Then write each one correctly.

7. _____
8. _____
9. _____
10. _____
11. _____
12. _____

> *Dearest Grandfather and Family,*
> *Mother and I have all ready reached Brooklyn, New York. We live in a building where alot of other people also live. Each family has an apartment that is there's alone. We have a cold white box with food that is already to cook, and theirs another box that washes our clothes. Father says that every one in Brooklyn lives like this!*
> *With love,*
> *Sixth Cousin*

WORKING WITH MEANING   Write a Spelling Word

to replace the underlined word or phrase in each sentence.

13. <u>Each</u> of the students was ready for the trip.
14. Is there <u>a chance at all</u> for us to leave earlier?
15. You may take the next train; <u>in any case</u>, the express train has left.
16. Is it <u>satisfactory</u> that I'm wearing western clothes?

13. _____
14. _____
15. _____
16. _____

COAST TO COAST "Pride of Puerto Rico:Roberto Clemente" and "In the Year of the Boar and Jackie Robinson" • Harcourt Brace School Publishers

Vocabulary WordShop

In "Pride of Puerto Rico: Roberto Clemente," the baseball star recalls that his first year with the Pittsburgh Pirates was a difficult one. Use Baseball Words to complete this sports announcer's comments about Clemente.

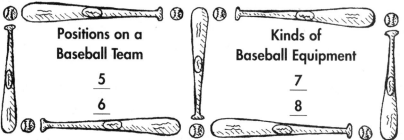

> There's Roberto Clemente, a new member of the **1**. He's so enthusiastic that he's already bowled over more than one **2** at the plate, just by running home.
>
> On the other hand, he's not much of an **3** yet. And why does a **4** bat for him so often? If he really has a bad back, as we've heard, why did the Pirates sign him?

Baseball
★ W O R D S ★

major leagues
outfielder
umpire
pinch hitter

SPELLING LOG How can you use the Baseball Words in your writing? Compose a sports story about baseball for your school or local newspaper. Add the words to your Spelling Log.

Think of other baseball words for team positions and objects associated with the sport. Write them on the lines at the left.

Positions on a Baseball Team	Kinds of Baseball Equipment
5	7
6	8

BASEBALL HOMOPHONES You may remember that homophones are words that sound alike but have different meanings and spellings. In each sentence an incorrect homphone has been used. Find it, think of the correct word, and write it on the corresponding line at the left.

9. The baseball players eight too much before the game.

10. Many players ran up and down the stares at the stadium.

11. Clemente ran so he'd be fast enough to steel bases.

12. At first it seamed strange to him to be away from home.

13. Soon Clemente's presents on the pitcher's mound became a real threat to batters on opposing teams.

14. After the World Series, Clemente finally felt at piece.

1. _____
2. _____
3. _____
4. _____

5. _____
6. _____
7. _____
8. _____

9. _____
10. _____
11. _____
12. _____
13. _____
14. _____

COAST TO COAST "Pride of Puerto Rico:Roberto Clemente" and "In the Year of the Boar and Jackie Robinson" • Harcourt Brace School Publishers

Name _____

WHAT'S IN A WORD?

After leaving the Pirates, Roberto Clemente played for the Dodgers, then based in Brooklyn, New York. How did this large industrial city ever get such a country-ish name? Actually, some seventeenth-century Dutch settlers named it for a city in Holland. The name *Brouckelen* means "broken land," a reference to its irregular coastline. Back then, fishing was excellent in the clean, clear waters of Brooklyn's coves and inlets.

1. Look up the names of some other United States cities. Choose one whose name you find interesting, and write a sentence to explain its origin. (The "geographical names" section in many dictionaries is a good place to look.)

DICTIONARY SKILLS Did you know that a dictionary can often tell you the language from which a word comes? Find some information on the place names below. Write the country or the language from which the word came.

2. Bronx (NY)   **3. New York (NY)**   **4. Charleston (SC)**

the Broncks

TROUBLESOME NO MORE! Make some flash cards for a quick review of the troublesome words and phrases in this lesson. Write each Spelling Word or phrase on one side of an index card and its meaning on the other side. Along with the meaning, include a sentence that illustrates how the word or phrase is used. Now choose one or two partners and practice the words. You might make a game out of it by taking turns spelling each word and giving its meaning. Or make up a second sentence showing each word's meaning. The longer you play, the better your review!

1. _____
_____
_____
_____
_____

2. _____
_____
_____
_____

3. _____
_____
_____
_____

4. _____
_____
_____
_____

Name _____

Practice Test

A. On the answer sheet, mark the letter of the underlined word that is spelled wrong in each sentence.

   Example: We once <u>livde</u> and <u>played</u> here.
                                   A   B

1. <u>Who's</u> <u>daughter</u> is she?
      A   B

2. This <u>canyon</u> is an <u>amazeing</u> place.
           A   B

3. I want a <u>dosen</u> <u>frozen</u> dinners.
            A   B

4. This <u>model</u> airplane has a <u>singel</u> engine.
         A   B

5. <u>Everyone</u> <u>cryed</u> at the end of the story.
      A   B

6. A lever <u>controlled</u> the toy <u>dragen</u>.
            A   B

7. We sat <u>all together</u> at the <u>formul</u> dinner.
          A   B

8. <u>Whose</u> the child who just <u>entered</u> the room?
     A   B

9. That <u>woman</u> has joined the city <u>counsil</u>.
       A   B

10. Suddenly I <u>remembered</u> what had <u>happend</u>.
           A   B

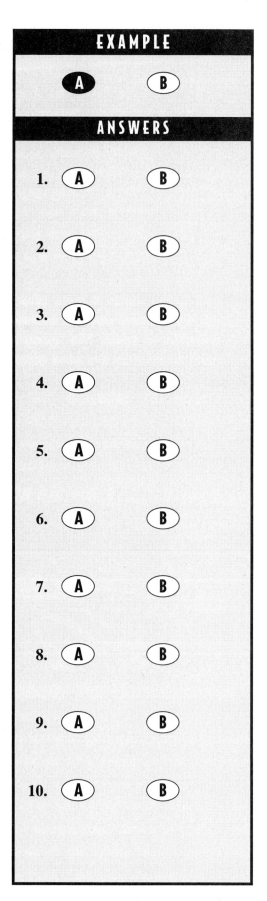

EXAMPLE

Ⓐ   Ⓑ

ANSWERS

1. Ⓐ   Ⓑ
2. Ⓐ   Ⓑ
3. Ⓐ   Ⓑ
4. Ⓐ   Ⓑ
5. Ⓐ   Ⓑ
6. Ⓐ   Ⓑ
7. Ⓐ   Ⓑ
8. Ⓐ   Ⓑ
9. Ⓐ   Ⓑ
10. Ⓐ   Ⓑ

B. Read the possible spellings for each word or expression. On the answer sheet, mark the letter of the correct spelling.

Example: A turnd   B ternd
           C terned   D turned

1. A practiceing   B practiseing
   C practicing   D pratising

2. A regretted   B regreted
   C rigreted   D rigretted

3. A flaver   B flavor
   C flayver   D flavir

4. A touer   B towor
   C tower   D towr

5. A doubel   B doubl
   C double   D dobbel

6. A trial   B tryal
   C tryle   D trile

7. A theirs   B thiers
   C thirs   D thers

8. A all rite   B all right
   C alrite   D all write

9. A leval   B levil
   C level   D levile

10. A visiting   B visting
    C vizting   D viseting

EXAMPLE

Ⓐ Ⓑ Ⓒ ●D

ANSWERS

1. Ⓐ Ⓑ Ⓒ Ⓓ
2. Ⓐ Ⓑ Ⓒ Ⓓ
3. Ⓐ Ⓑ Ⓒ Ⓓ
4. Ⓐ Ⓑ Ⓒ Ⓓ
5. Ⓐ Ⓑ Ⓒ Ⓓ
6. Ⓐ Ⓑ Ⓒ Ⓓ
7. Ⓐ Ⓑ Ⓒ Ⓓ
8. Ⓐ Ⓑ Ⓒ Ⓓ
9. Ⓐ Ⓑ Ⓒ Ⓓ
10. Ⓐ Ⓑ Ⓒ Ⓓ

Name _____

Unit 3: Writing Activities

WORDS TO WATCH FOR

staying
flowers
chalkboard
weak
seemed
going to
learned
thirty
tripped
anymore

Secret Celebrity Visits Concord School

Imagine that you've been chosen to write the news story about a famous person who visited your school. Choose the celebrity you'd like to see, and imagine the details of his or her visit. In your first paragraph, tell *who, what, when, where,* and *why* about the visit. In the next paragraph, give details describing the celebrity and telling the reactions of the students. Use as many Words to Watch For as you can.

Tips for Spelling Success

As you write your news story, watch for those troublesome words and phrases you studied in Lesson 16. If you think about the meanings of the words you use, you'll be sure to write them correctly!

Immigrants Who Have Made Names for Themselves

Tips for Spelling Success

Of course you'll remember to proofread the spelling of the immigrants' names. But then be sure to check the words used to tell about each one. Common verb endings are *-ate, -ize,* and *-fy.* Common adjective endings are *-al, -ive, -able,* and *-ary.*

Read a biography of someone who immigrated to the United States, perhaps *Baryshnikov: A Most Spectacular Dancer* by Saul Goodman. Then join a small group of classmates to discuss the immigrant you've each chosen. Work together to write five verbs and five adjectives that tell about each person. Then make a poster with a photo or drawing of each immigrant, and list the words you've written underneath.

$E=Mc^2$

COAST TO COAST Unit 3 Review • Harcourt Brace School Publishers

How to Grow the Best Corn Anywhere!

What do you do especially well? Care for pets? Organize games? Bake? Fix things? Grow plants? Write instructions for doing something you're good at and really know well. First, choose something simple with only a few steps, and write a title telling what you'll teach. List the materials needed, and then write the steps in the order in which you do them. End by describing your finished product.

Tips for Spelling Success

- Proofread your paragraph!
- Double-check the spellings of all materials or ingredients.
- If you used time-order words to show the order of steps, be sure they are spelled and punctuated correctly.

Mnemonics, Anyone?

From the lessons in this unit, choose some words whose spellings you find difficult to remember. Then join a group to work together on a few mnemonic clues, or memory aids, to help you remember them. Suppose *dietitian* is one of your words, and you must remember that it has two *t*'s. Try writing a sentence that emphasizes the two *t*'s. Here's a model:

Tips for Spelling Success

In addition to your mnemonics, try sounding out difficult words or associating them with words whose spellings you remember.

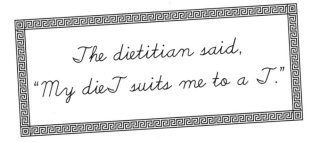

The dietitian said, "My dieT suits me to a T."

SPELLING ★ WORDS ★

1. capable
2. visible
3. terrible
4. suitable
5. reasonable
6. favorable
7. horrible
8. miserable
9. sensible
10. probable
11. available
12. remarkable
13. comfortable
14. responsible
15. valuable
16. considerable

Your Own ★ W O R D S ★

Look for other words that end in *-ible* and *-able* to add to the lists. You might see *perishable* or *flexible* on store signs.

17. _____
18. _____
19. _____
20. _____

Suffix: -ible/-able

These Spelling Words end in *-ible* or *-able*. Since the endings sound alike, you may need to memorize which word has which ending.

Sort the Spelling Words in a way that will help you remember them. One example word is given. Fill in the other one as you are sorting.

lovable

▶ The spelling of the base word may change when the suffix *-ible/-able* is added.

COAST TO COAST "Radio Fifth Grade" • Harcourt Brace School Publishers

Name _____

Strategy Workshop

PROOFREADING: Classifying Errors When you proofread, keep track of your spelling errors. Notice what kinds of mistakes you usually make, and work to correct them.

Proofread these words across the columns. Circle the misspelled words. Write all the words correctly on the lines.

1. availible   avalable   available
2. horible   horrible   horrable
3. favorable   favorible   favorble
4. visable   visible   visble
5. probable   probbible   probible
6. responsable   responsble   responsible
7. considerible   considrible   considerable

8–12. Proofread this script. Circle the misspelled words. Visualize their correct spellings. Write the words correctly.

Good morning, *'Kidsview'* listeners! Get comftible, because we have a valueable show today. First, our fitness expert offers workouts suitible for workout haters. Our science reporter has a remarkable preview of the next ice age. And Winston Churchill, our Mascot of the Week, treats you to some sensable parrot talk!

FUN WITH WORDS Write Spelling Words to complete this cartoon about Winston Churchill's problems.

This is __13__ ! He won't talk on the show!

He's __14__ of talking. He must be hungry. I'll get him some food!

No! Be __15__ ! Give him some water!

Hic! Hic! Splash! Hic!

Now he's __16__ — he's wet—and he has hiccups too!

1. ___ 2. ___ 3. ___ 4. ___ 5. ___ 6. ___ 7. ___ 8. ___ 9. ___ 10. ___ 11. ___ 12. ___ 13. ___ 14. ___ 15. ___ 16. ___

microphone
studio
producer
console

SPELLING LOG How might you use the Radio Production Words in your writing? Could you use them to write a television script? Add them to your Spelling Log.

1. Because
2. elephants
3. Kangaroo
4. Yabbadabbadoo

5. _____
6. _____
7. _____
8. _____
9. _____
10. _____

11. _____
    _____

Vocabulary WordShop

In "Radio Fifth Grade," Benjy Driver, producer of *Kidsview*, has an unbelievable day! Use the Radio Production Words to complete his thoughts.

I'm just here at the **1**, talking, and suddenly I'm on the floor doing push-ups! Arthur enters the **2** and starts raving about an ice age. Meanwhile, Mark and Ellen-Louise are cooling off a parrot with hiccups. And our engineer sits at his **3**, howling! Does every radio **4** have days like this?

Now think of other words that people at a radio station might need to know. Write them on the lines.

Radio Equipment	Radio Jobs	Radio Shows
5	7	9
6	8	10

WHAT'S IN A WORD?

Did you ever think about the word *radio*? It comes from the Latin word *radius*, which means "the spoke of a wheel," and it refers to the way radio signals travel. When the signals leave a radio station, they go to a high tower. The tower sends the signals out in all directions, like the spokes of a wheel.

11. **Why might radio signals also be called *radio waves*?**

Name _____

DICTIONARY SKILLS
When you look up the meaning of a word in a dictionary, read all the definitions. That way, you can choose the one that makes the most sense. On the lines, write a brief version of the best definition for each underlined word.

1. In a book about jobs for young people, you find *stand.*
   a. to remain unchanged
   b. a small structure used to sell things

2. In a photography book, you find *clear.*
   a. free from guilt or shame
   b. free of clouds or fog

3. In a book on U.S. Presidents, you find *run.*
   a. to enter or take part in a race or contest
   b. to operate a machine

4. In a math book, you find *answer.*
   a. to be responsible for something
   b. the solution to a problem

1. _____
2. _____
3. _____
4. _____

WORD HISTORIES
Many words begin with *per-*. Use a dictionary. On the lines, write only the words in which *per-* means "through." Leave the other lines blank.

5. persist   6. perennial

7. perish   8. permanent

9. perky   10. persecute

5. _____
6. _____
7. _____
8. _____
9. _____
10. _____

WHAT WAS THAT?
Form teams and play a game like charades. One person, who does not belong to a team, gives the Spelling Words to the players and acts as referee. Players take turns miming a word. Each time a word is guessed, the player who guesses successfully gets two points; then he or she must also spell the word correctly or lose a point. The team with the most points wins.

Name _____

Suffix: -ion

SPELLING ★ WORDS ★

1. nation
2. action
3. question
4. vacation
5. section
6. confusion
7. direction
8. attention
9. television
10. addition
11. permission
12. education
13. information
14. admission
15. celebration
16. instructions

A *suffix* is a word part added to the end of a word to change the way it is used. Each Spelling Word ends with the suffix *-ion* in one of its forms, *-sion* or *-tion*. Look at each word carefully. You will see that the spelling of the base word often changes when a suffix is added.

Sort the Spelling Words in a way that will help you remember them. One example word is given. Fill in the other one as you are sorting.

omission

Your Own WORDS

Look for other words with the suffix *-ion* to add to the lists. *Election* or *discussion* might be in a newspaper.

17. _____
18. _____
19. _____
20. _____

▶ When you add the suffix *-ion* (*-tion* or *-sion*) to a word, the spelling of the base word may change.

COAST TO COAST "By the Dawn's Early Light" • Harcourt Brace School Publishers

Strategy Workshop

SPELLING CLUES: Visualizing When you are learning to spell a word, study it carefully. Close your eyes and picture it spelled correctly. Then open your eyes and write the spelling you visualized.

Read these misspelled words. Visualize and then write the correct spellings. Check in a dictionary if you are not sure.

1. addision   2. admittion   3. directsion
4. attension   5. televition

6–11. Proofread these directions. Circle the misspellings, and write the correct spellings.

P lease follow these (instructions, instrucions) carefully so there will be no (confussion, confusion). First, if you are under the age of eighteen, ask a parent or guardian to fill in the (section, secshun) below. It gives you (permision, permission) to join the service. If you have a (question, qwestion) or need more (informtion, information), contact the commanding officer at Fort McHenry.

FUN WITH WORDS Complete the poem below using Spelling Words. The words in parentheses are clues.

After my short __12__ (schooling),
I will fight for our new __13__ (country).
When I am part of the __14__ (movement),
I will find much satisfaction.
We'll raise our flag in __15__ (festivity)
And take a well-deserved __16__ (time off).

1. _____
2. _____
3. _____
4. _____
5. _____

6. _____
7. _____
8. _____
9. _____
10. _____
11. _____

12. _____
13. _____
14. _____
15. _____
16. _____

COAST TO COAST "By the Dawn's Early Light" • Harcourt Brace School Publishers

Navy
★ WORDS ★

fleet
flagship
militia
ramparts

SPELLING LOG Think about how you might use these Navy Words in your writing. You could list them in your Spelling Log under Military Words. Could you use them in a report on the War of 1812?

1. _____
2. _____
3. _____
4. _____

5. _____
6. _____
7. _____
8. _____

9. _____
_____
_____
_____

Vocabulary WordShop

A young man wants to help the United States fight the British in the War of 1812. Write a Navy Word to complete each sentence about that war, below.

The British were well prepared to attack Baltimore because they had a large 1 of ships.

Sir Alexander Cochcrane, the British Vice Admiral, sailed on the 2 , which had eighty guns.

When the people of Baltimore found out that British ships would attack, they alerted their voluntary army, the 3 .

The citizens of Baltimore also built walls called 4 around their city to protect it.

Now think of other words that describe the Navy or another branch of the service. Write them on the lines at the left.

Navy Jobs	Navy Officers
5	7
6	8

WHAT'S IN A WORD?

The word *militia* comes from the Latin word *miles*, "a soldier," and refers to military service. A militia is composed of citizens with some military training who are available for local defense in an emergency. Militias were formed as long ago as 336 B.C. Later, during the American Revolution, the militia fought alongside the soldiers of the Continental Army. Today our militia is the National Guard.

9. Why do you think our colonial militia were called Minutemen?

COAST TO COAST "By the Dawn's Early Light" • Harcourt Brace School Publishers

Name _____

MULTIPLE MEANINGS Some everyday words have different meanings on a ship. Write words from the box to complete the sentences in the first group below. Then use the same words to complete sentences in the second group.

```
hold      cabin      hull      deck
```

1. The captain was asleep in his ___ .
2. The colonists stood on the ___ and watched the British ships approach.
3. The ship's ___ was damaged, and water poured in.
4. They stored the cargo in the ___ .

5. To play, we need a ___ of cards.
6. The ___ was built of logs.
7. May I ___ your puppy?
8. The ___ of this nut is hard to crack.

1. _____
2. _____
3. _____
4. _____
5. _____
6. _____
7. _____
8. _____

ANTHEM SEARCH Francis Scott Key wrote "The Star-Spangled Banner" as the British attacked Fort McHenry. Find and circle these words from the anthem in the puzzle: *bursting, perilous, glare, proudly, gleaming*. Write them on lines 9–13.

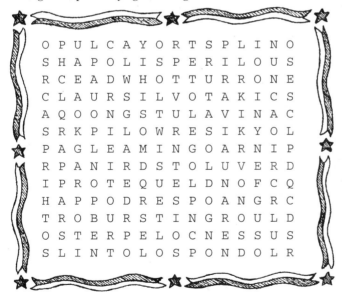

```
O P U L C A Y O R T S P L I N O
S H A P O L I S P E R I L O U S
R C E A D W H O T T U R R O N E
C L A U R S I L V O T A K I C S
A Q O O N G S T U L A V I N A C
S R K P I L O W R E S I K Y O L
P A G L E A M I N G O A R N I P
R P A N I R D S T O L U V E R D
I P R O T E Q U E L D N O F C Q
H A P P O D R E S P O A N G R C
T R O B U R S T I N G R O U L D
O S T E R P E L O C N E S S U S
S L I N T O L O S P O N D O L R
```

9. _____
10. _____
11. _____
12. _____
13. _____

SPELLING SLIPS Working with a classmate, write the Spelling Words on slips of paper. Put them in a box. One partner draws a slip and uses that word in a sentence, saying *blank* for the word. The classmate guesses the word and spells it correctly. Take turns until all the Spelling Words have been used.

Prefixes:
pre- **and** *pro-*

1. *predict*
2. *pretend*
3. *protect*
4. *preview*
5. *process*
6. *prevent*
7. *produce*
8. *prepare*
9. *product*
10. *program*
11. *provide*
12. *prefer*
13. *precaution*
14. *project*
15. *promised*
16. *previous*

Your Own ★ W O R D S ★

Look for other words with *pre-* and *pro-* to add to the lists. *Proceed* might be in a set of instructions.

17. _____
18. _____
19. _____
20. _____

A *prefix* is a word part placed before a base word or root to change the word's meaning. Each Spelling Word begins with the prefix *pre-* or *pro-*.

Sort the Spelling Words in a way that will help you remember them. One example word is given. Fill in the other one as you are sorting.

prescription

▶ The prefix *pre-* usually means "before." *Pro-* might mean "for" or "on behalf of." Both change the meaning of the base word or root.

COAST TO COAST "Yang the Youngest and His Terrible Ear" • Harcourt Brace School Publishers

Name _____

Strategy Workshop

PROOFREADING: Classifying Errors Instead of always making the same kinds of errors, keep a list of your misspellings. Classify them as *prefix errors, compound-word errors*, and so on. Study the list often to keep yourself aware of the kinds of mistakes you frequently make.

Circle the six misspelled words below. Follow the directions beneath the words to correct three kinds of spelling errors. Each direction applies to two words.

privious	proteck	predict	prepare
precuation	project	preveiw	produck
promised	prevent	prefer	prociss

1–2. Reverse two letters. Write the word correctly.
3–4. Change *i* to *e*. Write the word correctly.
5–6. Change the final consonant. Write the word correctly.

7–11. Proofread this invitation to a recital. Circle the five spelling errors. Write the words correctly.

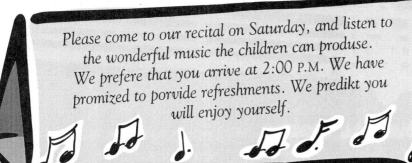

Please come to our recital on Saturday, and listen to the wonderful music the children can produse. We prefere that you arrive at 2:00 P.M. We have promized to porvide refreshments. We predikt you will enjoy yourself.

FUN WITH WORDS Write Spelling Words to replace 12–16.

I didn't **12** enough for my part in the **13** !

I'll play my violin and **14** to be you! The screen will **15** people from seeing me. This **16** will be a success!

1. _____
2. _____
3. _____
4. _____
5. _____
6. _____

7. _____
8. _____
9. _____
10. _____
11. _____
12. _____
13. _____
14. _____
15. _____
16. _____

Vocabulary WordShop

Pretend that a recital is being shown on television. It may be like the one in Lensey Namioka's story "Yang the Youngest and His Terrible Ear." You are the announcer. Write Music Recital Words to complete your comments.

Music Recital
★ WORDS ★

audience
violin
rhythm
composition

SPELLING LOG Think about how you might use these Music Recital Words in your writing. Could you use them to write a report about a great composer? Add them to your Spelling Log.

1. _____
2. _____
3. _____
4. _____

5. _____
6. _____
7. _____
8. _____

9. _____
10. _____
11. _____
12. _____
13. _____

It looks as though Yingtao is ready. He glances at the __1__ of family and friends and places his __2__ under his chin. Then he arranges the sheets of music printed with the __3__ he will play today. Folks, Yingtao looks nervous, but we're sure he'll do well if he can just remember the __4__ of the music.

5–8. Now think of other words to use for a music recital. Write them on the lines at the left.

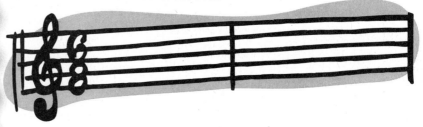

MUSICAL WORDS Many words that name musical instruments come from Italian. Use a dictionary with *etymologies,* or word origins, for the entry words. Match the name of each instrument with its definition or origin. Write the name of each instrument on the lines.

9. from *tromba,* the Italian word for a trumpet   a. tuba

10. short for *violoncello,* an instrument larger than a violin but smaller than a bass.   b. piccolo

11. short for *piccolo flauto,* "small flute"   c. trombone

12. plural of *timpano,* "kettledrum," a set of kettledrums played by one musician   d. timpani

13. the Italian word for a large, low-pitched brass instrument with a cone-shaped tube   e. cello

COAST TO COAST "Yang the Youngest and His Terrible Ear" • Harcourt Brace School Publishers

Name _____

WHAT'S IN A WORD?

Violins and fiddles are very much alike. The word *fiddle* was first used during the thirteenth century. *Violin*, from the Italian word *violino*, entered the English language during the sixteenth century. Both words meant "a stringed instrument played with a bow." Oddly enough, *vitula*, the Latin word on which both *fiddle* and *violin* are based, means "calf."

1. Explain how you know that the violin is played worldwide.

MORE RECITAL WORDS Use the words below to complete the fortune-cookie "fortunes." Use each word once.

> quartet   solo   sheet music   composer

2. Practice until you know every note in your ___

3. Without you, your ___ would be a trio!

4. The ___ of the music would be glad you're playing it.

5. All eyes will be on you during your ___ .

1. _____
_____
_____
_____
_____
_____
_____
_____
_____
_____

2. _____
3. _____
4. _____
5. _____

WORD SCRAMBLE Work with a partner. Divide the Spelling Words so you each have eight. On separate sheets of paper, you each write synonyms for your words. Then trade papers, and write Spelling Words that match the synonyms on your partner's list. Trade papers again to see whether your partner wrote the words you had in mind. Check each other's spelling!

Name _____

COAST TO COAST "A Very Young Musician" • Harcourt Brace School Publishers

SPELLING ★ WORDS ★

1. return
2. relax
3. invited
4. uncover
5. remind
6. invented
7. uneasy
8. include
9. review
10. unknown
11. interrupt
12. interview
13. unpleasant
14. intermediate
15. rehearse
16. recital

Your Own ★ WORDS ★

Look for other words with the prefixes *un-*, *re-*, *in-*, and *inter-* to add to your lists. *Information* or *research* might be found in a language arts textbook.

17. _____
18. _____
19. _____
20. _____

Prefixes: *un-*, *re-*, *in-*, and *inter-*

You may remember that a prefix is a word part placed before a base word or root to change its meaning. Each of these Spelling Words begins with *un-*, *re-*, *in-*, or *inter-*.

Sort the Spelling Words in a way that will help you remember them. You may want to group them by their prefixes.

▶ The prefix *re-* means "again," and *un-* usually means "not." *In-* may mean "in," "into," or "upon." *Inter-* usually means "between." All of these prefixes will change the meanings of base words or roots.

Strategy Workshop

PROOFREADING: Dictionary Skills The guide words at the top of each dictionary page can help you quickly find a word. The words below in brackets are guide words. Use them to look up each misspelled Spelling Word in the Spelling Dictionary. Then write the words correctly.

1. [however knight] envited   2. [however knight] intermedate
3. [treasure violin] uncuver   4. [however knight] inklude
5. [treasure violin] uneazy   6. [however knight] interveiw

7–12. To complete this thank-you note, replace each pair of guide words with a word from the Spelling Dictionary. Find the page on which the guide words appear. Choose the Spelling Word on that page that best fits the corresponding sentence in the thank-you note. Write the word correctly.

> *You often have to (however knight) my lesson and (rather riot) me what to do. Thanks for being patient, especially when I'm (treasure violin). I promise to (rather riot) my lessons more often.*
>
> *At a (rather riot), I always (rather riot) since you've taught me well. Thanks for all your help!*

1. _____
2. _____
3. _____
4. _____
5. _____
6. _____

7. _____
8. _____
9. _____
10. _____
11. _____
12. _____

FUN WITH WORDS Write Spelling Words to replace 13-16.

Now my trumpet is dented! Why was it ever 13 ?
I asked my mom to 14 it. It's so hard to learn it!
I feel worse and worse when it's time to 15 .
I groan and I groan, but for reasons 16
My mom just keeps saying, "My child, keep playing."

13. _____
14. _____
15. _____
16. _____

Musical Instrument ★ WORDS ★

brass
woodwind
percussion
piano

SPELLING LOG Think about how you might use the Musical Instrument Words in your writing. Would they help if you were writing about choosing a musical instrument? Add them to your Spelling Log.

1. _____
2. _____
3. _____
4. _____

5. _____
6. _____
7. _____
8. _____
9. _____
10. _____

Vocabulary WordShop

Imagine you are a salesperson in a store that sells musical instruments. Josh Broder, the boy in Jill Krementz's "A Very Young Musician," might come by for trumpet music. But wait! Here comes someone now! Use the Musical Instrument Words to show what you will say to him or her.

Do you want to play in the _1_ section? This trumpet is just the thing for you! Something smaller? How about this piccolo from the _2_ group? Well, if you really want to get people's attention, you need a drum from the _3_ group! If you don't want to be in the marching band, then I've got a really great _4_ , just for you!

Now think of the names of other instruments that would belong under the headings below. Write them at the left.

Fred's Music Store

STRINGED INSTRUMENTS
_5_
_6_

BRASS INSTRUMENTS
_7_
_8_

WOODWIND INSTRUMENTS
_9_
_10_

Name _____

WHAT'S IN A WORD?

The name *piano* is a kind of nickname! The original word for this instrument was *gravicembalo col piano e forte*, an Italian phrase for "harpsichord with soft and loud." Its name was first shortened to *piano e forte*, then to *pianoforte*, and finally to *piano*, which actually means "soft."

1. Name some books in which people, animals, or objects have nicknames.

ANALOGIES   In an analogy, two pairs of words have the same or a similar relationship to each other, as in *Make* is to *create* as *complete* is to *finish*. Here the words in each pair are synonyms. Complete each analogy below with a word from the box. Use a dictionary if you need help.

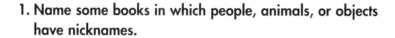

| tempo | concert | baton | conductor |

2. *Worker* is to *employee* as *leader* is to___.

3. *Volume* is to *loudness* as *speed* is to___.

4. *Shepherd* is to *staff* as *conductor* is to___.

5. *Painting* is to *exhibit* as *music* is to ___.

1. _____
_____
_____
_____
_____

2. _____
3. _____
4. _____
5. _____

SELF-CHECK   Work with a partner. List the eight Spelling Words that are hardest for you to learn. Then trade lists with your partner, and see whether you listed any of the same words. Put the lists aside for a while. Then have your partner read your difficult words aloud as you spell them. Do the same for him or her. Have you mastered your biggest challenges?

Integrated Spelling

SPELLING ★ WORDS ★

1. decided
2. details
3. discount
4. design
5. degree
6. demand
7. disturbed
8. develop
9. disadvantage
10. describe
11. disability
12. delight
13. disappointed
14. defense
15. dissatisfied
16. deduct

Your Own WORDS

Look for other words with the prefixes *dis-* and *de-* to add to the lists. You might find *destroy* or *disorder* in a history textbook.

17. _____
18. _____
19. _____
20. _____

Prefixes: *dis-* and *de-*

You may remember that a prefix is a word part placed before a base word or root to change its meaning. Each Spelling Word begins with the prefix *dis-* or the prefix *de-*.

Sort the Spelling Words in a way that will help you remember them. You may want to group them by their prefixes.

displeased

_____
_____
_____
_____
_____
_____

defer

_____
_____
_____
_____
_____
_____
_____
_____

▶ The prefix *dis-* often means "not" or "the opposite of."
▶ The prefix *de-* can mean "from," "down," "off," "away," "of," or "out."

COAST TO COAST "Beethoven Lives Upstairs" • Harcourt Brace School Publishers

Integrated Spelling

Strategy Workshop

PROOFREADING: Comparing Spellings When you are proofreading, it is sometimes helpful to write a word in more than one way. Then you can compare the spellings and choose the word that looks right to you.

Study the words across the columns. Decide which spellings look right. Circle incorrect spellings. Write the correct ones.

1. delite	deligte	delight
2. disappointed	disuppointed	diseppointed
3. disubilety	disability	disebelity
4. disavantage	disadvantage	disedvantege
5. disatisfied	dissatisfyed	dissatisfied
6. describe	discribe	discrybe

1. _____
2. _____
3. _____
4. _____
5. _____
6. _____

7–12. Read this letter. Search for words that look wrong and circle them. On scratch paper, write these words in different ways. Choose the ones that look right. Write them on the lines.

Dear Uncle,
What a problem has begun to divelop at our house! Mother disided to rent out Father's upstairs office, and a madman has moved in. I cannot give you all the detayles, but for both our sakes I dimand that you talk to Mother! Already she has had to deeduct money from his rent to pay for house repairs. This just can't go on. Please come to my difence!

7. _____
8. _____
9. _____
10. _____
11. _____
12. _____

FUN WITH WORDS Use the Spelling Words to complete this description of a young man studying to be a musician.

He has a great deal of talent, but very little money, so he buys what he needs at a __13__ store. Once he tried to __14__ a plan for his studies so he'd get his __15__ in three years. It could have saved him a lot of money. So it __16__ him greatly that he had to follow the schedule like everyone else.

13. _____
14. _____
15. _____
16. _____

Name _____

Symphony
★ WORDS ★

musician
sopranos
orchestras
tenors

SPELLING LOG Think about how you might use these Symphony Words in your writing. Add them to your Spelling Log.

1. _____
2. _____
3. _____
4. _____

5. _____
6. _____
7. _____
8. _____

9. _____
_____
_____
_____

Vocabulary WordShop

Imagine that you're the music critic for a local newspaper. Like Christoph in "Beethoven Lives Upstairs," you have just attended a performance of Beethoven's Ninth Symphony. Use the Symphony Words to complete your article for the newspaper.

I'm sure that _1_ all over the world will soon be playing this wonderful symphony! The _2_ were delighted with the effects of their high notes. The _3_ in the men's chorus seemed pleased with their parts as well. In fact, every _4_ on the stage and every person in the audience seemed to realize that history was being made!

Now think of other words you might use to describe a symphony. Write them on the lines.

Kinds of Melodies	Kinds of Instruments
5	7
6	8

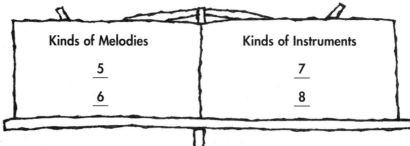

WHAT'S IN A WORD?

The ancient Greeks believed that music and many other arts were inspired by nine goddesses. These goddesses, all sisters, were called the Muses. At first, the Greek word mousikē referred to any art inspired by the Muses, including poetry, song and dance, comedy, and astronomy. By the time this word entered the English language, the term music referred only to a pleasing arrangement of tones.

9. Write at least three other words that come from the word music or from the word muse, which now means "to become absorbed in thought."

Name _____

DEPENDING ON DICTIONARIES
A dictionary can help you spell, pronounce, and use a word correctly. Study these dictionary entries, and answer the questions below. If you need a pronunciation key, look in your Spelling Dictionary.

Entry Word: Dots divide the entry word into syllables.

Pronunciation: The letters, symbols, and accent marks that appear between brackets show how to say the word. A key lists the sound for each symbol.

Definitions: If there is more than one meaning, each meaning is numbered.

mu•si•cian [myoo̅·zish´ən] *n.* A person who is skilled in music, especially a professional composer or performer of music.

so•pran•o [sə·pran´ō] *n., pl.* **so•pran•os**
1 *adj.* Having a high or the highest range, as a voice or instrument. **2** *n.* A soprano voice.
3 *n.* A singer with such a voice.

1. For *musician,* which syllable is stressed, or accented—the first, the second, or the third?
2. For *soprano,* which of the meanings is a noun, 1 or 2?
3. Write a sentence about two people who sing the soprano part of a musical composition. Use the correct plural form of *soprano* in the sentence.
4. According to the definitions above, is a soprano a musician? How do you know?

1. _____

2. _____

3. _____

_____

_____

_____

4. _____

_____

_____

_____

CUT-UPS
Work with a partner. Write each Spelling Word in the center of an index card. Then cut each card in two pieces, cutting in a straight line between the prefix and the root or base word. Place the halves upside down, and use them to play Concentration. Take turns flipping over two halves. If you find two that form a Spelling Word, keep them. Whether or not you find a match, the other person takes a turn. See how many turns it takes both of you to match all the halves.

Integrated Spelling

Onomatopoeia

COAST TO COAST "Beetles, Lightly Toasted" and "Have a Happy..." • Harcourt Brace School Publishers

SPELLING
★ WORDS ★

1. rattle
2. grind
3. splash
4. honked
5. slurp
6. roaring
7. crackling
8. gurgle
9. rustling
10. sizzle
11. creaking
12. squeak
13. trickled
14. chattering
15. squawked
16. murmur

Your Own
★ WORDS ★

Look for other words that imitate sounds, and add them to your lists. You might find *buzzing* or *hissing* in a science textbook.

17. _____
18. _____
19. _____
20. _____

The Spelling Words are all examples of *onomatopoeia*, which means that they imitate sounds. Sort them in a way that will help you remember them. Four categories are given.

water sounds

fire sounds

animal sounds

other sounds

▶ Some words imitate sounds in the environment.

Strategy Workshop

PROOFREADING: Comparing Spellings If you cannot remember how to spell a word, try writing it several ways. Then choose the spelling that looks right to you.

Each line below has three spellings of the same word. Circle the misspelled words. Then write the correct spelling.

1. squeek	squaek	squeak
2. rooring	roering	roaring
3. chatering	chattering	chatturing
4. honcked	honnked	honked
5. skwaked	squawked	skuawked
6. rattle	ratle	rattel

7–12. This paragraph is a draft of an essay mentioned in "Beetles, Lightly Toasted." Proofread it carefully. Circle the misspelled words, and write the correct spellings.

> How Insects and Worms Can Save Money and the Food Supply
> We all slerp food, but we don't think about conserving it. I can get rid of a few rusling insects and save money as well. Yes, I can grinde up beetles and use them like walnuts. I can spash worms into hot oil and cook them until they sizzel. When people taste them, they will mermer, "How good!" But this happens only if they don't know what we're cooking!

FUN WITH WORDS Use the Spelling Words to replace 13–16.

1. _____
2. _____
3. _____
4. _____
5. _____
6. _____

7. _____
8. _____
9. _____
10. _____
11. _____
12. _____

13. _____
14. _____
15. _____
16. _____

This brownie is so crunchy that it makes a __13__ sound every time I chew.

Cool! And I can hear this milk __14__ in my stomach when I drink it!

This juice __15__ down my throat just right. It really cooled me off!

Well, while you drank it, you missed the sound of my bones __16__. Must be growing pains!

Name _____

Vocabulary WordShop

SPELLING LOG Think about how you might use these Craft Words in your writing. Then add them to your Spelling Log.

1. _____
2. _____
3. _____
4. _____

5. _____
6. _____
7. _____
8. _____

9. _____
10. _____
11. _____
12. _____
13. _____
14. _____
15. _____
16. _____
17. _____
18. _____

In "Have a Happy . . ." Chris makes several things from wood. Use the Craft Words to show his thoughts.

What kind of _1_ can I make with this clothespin? Usually it's a _2_ to hold wet clothes on a line, but I can think of a new use. When my family sees this, they'll say, "What a _3_ !" Maybe the _4_ will be on TV!

Think of some other words for items that people make by hand. Write your words on the lines.

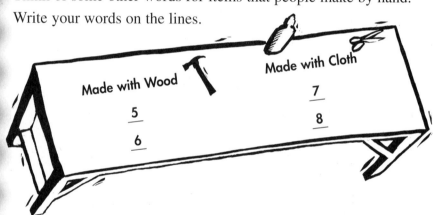

Made with Wood
5 ___
6 ___

Made with Cloth
7 ___
8 ___

DID YOU HEAR THAT WORD? Hidden in this puzzle are ten more words that imitate sounds. Circle each word you find, and then write them all on the lines at the right.

```
A G I G G L E H E B A L T U R O
R E S P A L O G A U S R O A V O E
O R D A T U M S C R E E C H A L E
Q U E S K E R T R S A T O V L C T
U S I V Q U R U S T L E E S U T P
E H O A L U T H O R C E N O L A C
W O R S I N E E N T U L P R A C S
R I G H P O V A T C P O P L I S
S C R A S H O R L V E R S P O K K
H O U C O M P L W T T V I L N O
```

Name _____

WHAT'S IN A WORD?

Chris learns some Swahili when his family celebrates Kwanzaa, a new-year festival. Many English words came from Africa. For example, the words *okra*, a green vegetable, and *gumbo*, a kind of stew, are from West Africa. So are *banjo*, a stringed musical instrument, *tote*, meaning "to carry," and *yam*, a vegetable like a sweet potato.

1. In the library, use a French-English dictionary, or a similar book for another language. Look up three words from the other language. Write each word you looked up and what it means in English.

1. _____
_____
_____
_____
_____

MORE WORDS FROM OTHER LANGUAGES

Match each word, below left, with the language it came from, below right. Write the letters of the languages on the lines. Use a dictionary if you need to.

Word	Language
2. raccoon	a. Italian
3. chef	b. French
4. prima donna	c. Algonquian
5. dandelion	
6. pasta	
7. moccasin	

2. _____
3. _____
4. _____
5. _____
6. _____
7. _____

IT SOUNDS LIKE . . . Divide the Spelling Words with a partner so you each have eight words. Write a one-line description of something that might make the noise named in each of your words. An example for *bubble* might be "sounds like a pot boiling." Then trade descriptions. Write the Spelling Word that matches each of your partner's clues.

Practice Test

A. Read each sentence. On the answer sheet, mark the answer that indicates whether the underlined word is spelled right or wrong.

Example: I could hear the package <u>rattel</u>.

1. Was the report <u>favorable</u>?

2. The flag was raised in <u>selebration</u>.

3. It takes practice to <u>produse</u> clear notes.

4. A musician must <u>reherse</u> for hours.

5. The militia had clear <u>instructions</u>.

6. Tell me all the <u>detales</u>.

7. Beetles make a <u>crackling</u> sound when you grind them.

8. Who is <u>responsable</u> for this radio program?

9. The <u>previous</u> performer had done well.

10. Beethoven was not to be <u>disturbed</u>.

EXAMPLE

◯ RIGHT ⬤ WRONG

ANSWERS

1. ◯ RIGHT ◯ WRONG

2. ◯ RIGHT ◯ WRONG

3. ◯ RIGHT ◯ WRONG

4. ◯ RIGHT ◯ WRONG

5. ◯ RIGHT ◯ WRONG

6. ◯ RIGHT ◯ WRONG

7. ◯ RIGHT ◯ WRONG

8. ◯ RIGHT ◯ WRONG

9. ◯ RIGHT ◯ WRONG

10. ◯ RIGHT ◯ WRONG

COAST TO COAST Unit 4 Review • Harcourt Brace School Publishers

Name _____

B. Read each group of words. Find the underlined word that is misspelled. On the answer sheet, mark the letter of that word.

Example: A take <u>action</u>   B door <u>creaking</u>
           C science <u>projeck</u>   D big <u>discount</u>

1. A <u>valuable</u> lesson   B teeth <u>chattering</u>
    C <u>roreing</u> fire   D <u>unpleasant</u> smell

2. A <u>available</u> time   B <u>uneazy</u> feeling
    C <u>dissatisfied</u> customer   D growing <u>murmur</u>

3. A pay <u>atention</u>   B you <u>promised</u>
    C <u>sensible</u> shoes   D <u>deduct</u> taxes

4. A good <u>information</u>   B strong <u>defens</u>
    C <u>prepare</u> dinner   D <u>remind</u> him

5. A movie <u>preview</u>   B <u>horrible</u> day
    C free <u>admission</u>   D tiny <u>skweek</u>

6. A <u>comfortible</u> jeans   B start to <u>gurgle</u>
    C at a <u>disadvantage</u>   D <u>return</u> to base

7. A <u>interrupt</u> you   B take a <u>precaution</u>
    C complicated <u>desine</u>   D <u>probable</u> victory

8. A <u>slurp</u> a milkshake   B <u>visable</u> line
    C <u>unknown</u> person   D good <u>question</u>

9. A <u>invented</u> something   B <u>describe</u> yourself
    C <u>predict</u> a storm   D <u>rusling</u> leaves

10. A give <u>permision</u>   B <u>considerable</u> cost
     C <u>interview</u> me   D slight <u>disability</u>

EXAMPLE

(A) (B) ●C (D)

ANSWERS

1. (A) (B) (C) (D)

2. (A) (B) (C) (D)

3. (A) (B) (C) (D)

4. (A) (B) (C) (D)

5. (A) (B) (C) (D)

6. (A) (B) (C) (D)

7. (A) (B) (C) (D)

8. (A) (B) (C) (D)

9. (A) (B) (C) (D)

10. (A) (B) (C) (D)

COAST TO COAST Unit 4 Review • Harcourt Brace School Publishers

Name _____

Unit 4: Writing Activities

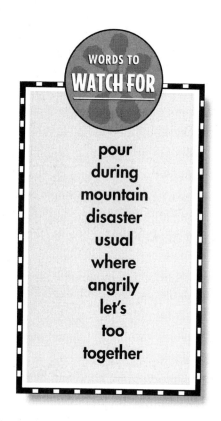

pour
during
mountain
disaster
usual
where
angrily
let's
too
together

A Musical Miracle

Have you ever wished that you could play a certain musical instrument? Write about a person who can play this instrument with great skill. Include some Words to Watch For in your story. Begin by describing the character's efforts to play. Show how he or she tries and fails, again and again. But don't let your character give up. Later, describe his or her happiness at being able to play. Have a partner read your first draft and suggest changes, such as ways to emphasize your character's refusal to give up.

Tips for Spelling Success

If you're unsure of the spelling or meaning of a word, consult a dictionary. Use the guide words at the top of the dictionary page to help you find it quickly.

Tips for Spelling Success

- Be sure you've spelled the musician's name correctly, as well as the examples you give.
- Check the spelling of the person's town and country, if you mentioned them.
- Use a dictionary to verify the spellings of instruments.

A Different Kind of Musical Note

Who is your favorite musician or composer? Francis Scott Key? Beethoven? Wynton Marsalis? Write a letter to him or her (even if the person is no longer alive). Explain why you like his or her music, and give examples of songs or compositions that you especially like.

COAST TO COAST Unit 4 Review • Harcourt Brace School Publishers

Integrated Spelling

Hear Here!

Read three short articles about a musician or performer whose work you like. Encyclopedia entries, magazine articles, and even CD cases and old album covers are all good sources. Jot down a few facts that you've learned from your reading. Then bring your notes and a photo from an album or CD cover to school. Join four or five classmates and show them the photo. Use your notes to discuss what you've read, comparing your performer's work with that of your classmates' choices. Finally, display your notes and photo on a "musical" bulletin board.

Tips for Spelling Success

Be sure to proofread the spelling of your performer's name and the information in your notes before displaying them.

Rhyming Riddles

Do the students in your school like riddles? If so, make up several riddles with rhyming answers. Here is an example:

Q: What do you call a bad gift?

A: An unpleasant present!

After you and your classmates share your riddles, tape-record the funniest ones to keep in the classroom library. You may also want to make a book of riddles to go with the tape.

Tips for Spelling Success

- If you have a list of Rhyming Words in your Spelling Log, check it for riddle ideas.

- Remember that the *sounds* of the words make the rhymes, not their spellings.

- Check to see that you've spelled the rhyming words correctly.

Spelling Patterns: VCCV Words

1. window
2. circus
3. appear
4. tennis
5. survive
6. object
7. effort
8. fellow
9. welcome
10. narrow
11. office
12. afford
13. members
14. forward
15. common
16. support

Your Own WORDS

Look for other words with the VCCV spelling pattern, and add them to the lists. You might see *banner* or *distance* in the sports section of the newspaper.

17. _____
18. _____
19. _____
20. _____

Each Spelling Word includes a vowel, two consonants together, and then another vowel. Each word also has two syllables.

Sort the Spelling Words according to which syllable is accented. Two example words are given. One Spelling Word can fit into both lists, depending on how it is used.

hammer

mistake

▶ In most words with the VCCV pattern, the syllable break occurs between the two consonants in the middle of the word.

▶ In VCCV words, the accent may be on the first syllable or the second syllable.

COAST TO COAST "The American Family Farm" • Harcourt Brace School Publishers

Integrated Spelling

Name _____

Strategy Workshop

SPELLING CLUES: Listening Carefully When you are unsure of the spelling of a two-syllable word, say the word and listen to the way each syllable sounds. Think of the spelling patterns that make the sounds. Then write the word.

Say the syllables in each word below, and listen to their sounds. Write the word that sounds correct.

1. survive	suvive	2. fellow	feelow
3. cirecus	circus	4. tennis	tinis
5. willcome	welcome	6. foward	forward

7–13. Proofread this list. Circle each misspelled word. Then write the words correctly.

> *Equipment that we can aford this year:*
> *a new tractor with a nawrow turning radius*
> *a hay baler that will apere new even if used*
> *a new typewriter for the farm ofise*
> *a wendow to replace the broken one in the house*
> *a riding mower that doesn't take much efurt to use*
> *a sign or other obbject with our address on it*
> *(to place near the road)*

FUN WITH WORDS Use the Spelling Words to complete the sentence.

The 14 of the farmers' co-op association give each other 15 because they have 16 roots.

1. _____
2. _____
3. _____
4. _____
5. _____
6. _____

7. _____
8. _____
9. _____
10. _____
11. _____
12. _____
13. _____

14. _____
15. _____
16. _____

Farm
★ WORDS ★

agriculture
pastureland
livestock
silo

SPELLING LOG Think about using Farm Words in your writing. They may be helpful in a science report. Add them to your Spelling Log.

1. _____
2. _____
3. _____
4. _____

5. _____
6. _____
7. _____
8. _____
9. _____
10. _____

11. _____
_____
_____
_____
_____
_____

Vocabulary WordShop

In "The American Family Farm," Willie and Linda Adams list some questions they have for the members of their farmers' co-op association. Use Farm Words to complete the list.

1. Can anyone use the corn that won't fit into our ____?
2. Is there any extra ____ for cattle close to our farm?
3. Which crops do the experts on ____ suggest for next year?
4. Can we trade ____? We have too many goats but need more cattle.

Now think of other words you might associate with a farm or farm work. These headings may help you think of some.

Machines	Buildings	Crops
5	7	9
6	8	10

WHAT'S IN A WORD?

For most of us, the phrases *down-to-earth* and *grass roots* recall a time in which people led a simpler life. *Down-to-earth* means "practical," whereas *grass roots* refers to something basic, part of the foundation of our society. Both arose in the farming communities of the late nineteenth and early twentieth centuries, when farm living stood for hard work, honesty, and family.

Today we often add "refreshing" and "healthful" to our idea of grass roots. Maybe we'd all like to slow down a little!

11. What do politicians mean when they say they are starting a campaign at the "grass roots" of society?

COAST TO COAST "The American Family Farm" • Harcourt Brace School Publishers

Name _____

IDIOMS An idiom is made up of ordinary words that take on an additional meaning when they are used together. The idioms below were used in "The American Family Farm." Write the correct idiom in each sentence.

----

common roots   old days   hard times   work the land

----

1. Many people are drawn together by their ___.
2. ___ happen whenever people have trouble finding jobs.
3. Grandparents often remind children and grandchildren of the problems they faced in the ___.
4. Few of us ___ today, since most people live in urban areas.

YOUNG ANIMAL WORDS Write the correct responses. To make this activity into a game, form teams and list additional "young animal words."

A young cow is a __5__ .   A young goose is a __10__ .
A young deer is a __6__ .   A young goat is a __11__ .
A young sheep is a __7__ .   A young bear is a __12__ .
A young horse is a __8__ .   A young pig is a __13__ .
A young duck is a __9__ .   A young cat is a __14__ .

VCCV VOLLEY Play this game with a partner. Divide the Spelling Words between you. Each of you should write clue sentences for your eight words. Each sentence should give a clue to the word's meaning, without using the word.

Then take turns. One partner reads aloud a clue sentence, and the other guesses and spells the Spelling Word that fits the clue. The guesser may take a quick look at the list of Spelling Words if he or she is stumped. Exchange roles after each word.

1. _____
2. _____
3. _____
4. _____

5. _____
6. _____
7. _____
8. _____
9. _____
10. _____
11. _____
12. _____
13. _____
14. _____

Name _____

Spelling Patterns: VCCCV Words

Each Spelling Word is a two-syllable word that includes a vowel, three consonants together, and then another vowel. The syllable break almost always comes between two of the middle consonants. Sometimes the two middle consonants that fall in the same syllable make a single sound, such as *th* or *ch*. Sometimes they form a cluster in which you can hear the sounds of both letters, such as *cr* or *pl*.

Sort the Spelling Words in a way that will help you remember them.

perchance

monster

▶ To spell a two-syllable word that has three consonants in the middle, divide the word into syllables. If the two consonants form a cluster or make a single sound, divide the word before or after those two consonants. Then spell the word, one syllable at a time.

SPELLING ★ WORDS ★

1. farther
2. explode
3. extra
4. merchant
5. improve
6. orchard
7. ostrich
8. display
9. instead
10. purchase
11. increase
12. panther
13. Congress
14. although
15. complex
16. portrait

Your Own ★ WORDS ★

Look for other words spelled with the VCCCV pattern and add them to the lists. You might find *subtract* and *explain* in a math textbook.

17. _____
18. _____
19. _____
20. _____

COAST TO COAST "Amish Home" • Harcourt Brace School Publishers

Name _____

Strategy Workshop

SPELLING CLUES: Little Words To help yourself remember how to spell a word of two or more syllables, check to see if the word includes a little word that you already know how to spell. Then you'll have a head start!

Write the Spelling Word in which each of these smaller words can be found.

1. pan	2. far	3. chant
4. port	5. rich	6. play

7–12. Proofread this list of a farmer's goals for the year. Circle the misspelled words. Write the words correctly.

Goals for the Coming Year
- Add ektra fertilizer to north field to impruve crop.
- Porchase new harness for lead horse.
- Increese size of orcherd.
- Replace buggy tires before they explod.

WORKING WITH MEANING Write Spelling Words to replace 13–16.

Compared to an Amish farm, __13__ is very __14__. Yet the Amish could help many others use resources wisely. __15__ their lives are simple, they enjoy themselves. __16__ of material things, they have each other.

1. _____
2. _____
3. _____
4. _____
5. _____
6. _____

7. _____
8. _____
9. _____
10. _____
11. _____
12. _____

13. _____
14. _____
15. _____
16. _____

Amish-Related ★ WORDS ★

practical

agrarian

respectful

devout

SPELLING LOG Think about how to use the Amish-Related Words in your writing. Add them to your Spelling Log.

1. _____
2. _____
3. _____
4. _____

5. _____
6. _____
7. _____
8. _____
9. _____
10. _____

_____
_____
_____
_____
_____
_____
_____
_____

Vocabulary WordShop

In "Amish Home," we learn that Amish people who came to the American colonies lived as many others did. Back then, farming was the way that families fed and clothed themselves. Use Amish-Related Words to complete this report.

In those early days, many families had farms and lived an __1__ life. Food and other things were scarce, so people had to be __2__ and not waste the little they had. They learned to be __3__ of the land because they depended on it. And because their religious beliefs were important to them, many people, the Amish included, were __4__ as well.

5–10. Now think of other words that might describe the Amish. Write them on the lines at the left.

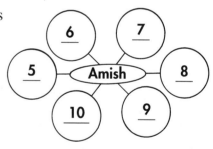

WHAT I ADMIRE The Amish live simpler, quieter lives than most of us do. Choose an Amish-Related Word or one of the words you wrote for your word web. Describe in two sentences something you admire about these people.

Name _____

WHAT'S IN A WORD?

The words *agrarian* and *agriculture* both come from the Latin root *ager*, "field." And both share their histories with the word *acre.*

Back in the thirteenth century, an acre was just any old field. But when Edward I became king of England in 1272, all that changed. He ordered a farmer with a team of oxen to begin plowing early in the morning. At the end of the day, he measured the newly plowed land, which covered an area 40 poles long by 4 poles wide. "That," said King Edward, "is an acre."

Today, an acre is still 40 poles long by 4 poles wide. Only we say that it's 43,560 square feet.

1. Explain why most of the stories grouped under the theme "Planet of Life" could be called "agrarian."

1. _____
_____
_____

HOMOPHONES   Homophones are words that have different meanings and spellings but are pronounced the same way. Sometimes only *parts* of words sound the same, which can be confusing. Study the two definitions for each word. Write the correct definition for each one. Check a dictionary if you wish.

2. prevail   **a. to come before a veil**
                b. to persist

3. adhere   **a. to be loyal**
                b. to be able to hear

4. fluorescent **a. sent by the florist**
                b. glowing brightly

5. bale   **a. to pump water out of a boat**
                b. a large bundle

2. _____
3. _____
4. _____
5. _____

TWO GUESSES   Work with a partner to play this spelling game. Each partner has a list of the Spelling Words to use. Take turns giving clues for a particular word. For example, say, "I am thinking of a word that means 'a picture.' You have two guesses." Your partner tries to identify the word, in this case *portrait,* in one or two guesses and then spells it. Continue until both of you have correctly spelled all the words.

Name _____

Spelling Patterns: VCV Words

Each Spelling Word has two syllables and is spelled with a single consonant between two vowel sounds. In all the words, the first syllable is accented. Sometimes the vowel sound in the first syllable is long, and sometimes it is short.

Sort the Spelling Words in a way that will help you remember them.

V/CV
laser

_____
_____
_____
_____
_____
_____
_____
_____

VC/V
olive

_____
_____
_____
_____
_____
_____
_____
_____

▶ If the vowel sound in the first syllable is long, the syllable break comes before the consonant (V/CV).

▶ If the vowel sound in the first syllable is short, the syllable break comes after the consonant (VC/V).

SPELLING ★ WORDS ★

1. robin
2. travel
3. even
4. peanut
5. moment
6. chosen
7. private
8. stolen
9. item
10. solid
11. vacant
12. balance
13. finish
14. basin
15. minutes
16. desert

Your Own ★ WORDS ★

Look for other words with the VCV pattern and add them to the lists. You might find *finance* and *crisis* in the newspaper.

17. _____
18. _____
19. _____
20. _____

Strategy Workshop

PROOFREADING: Comparing Spellings When you are proofreading, sometimes it is helpful to write a word in more than one way. Then you can compare the spellings and choose the word that looks right to you.

Study these word pairs. Write the Spelling Words.

1. ballance   balance   2. solid   solled

3. idem   item   4. robben   robin

5. private   pryvit   6. basin   basen

7–13. Read each pair of words in parentheses on the poster. Write the correctly spelled word in each set.

Stop for a (moment, momment)! Don't (evin, even) think of cutting down our trees! If you do, you will (finish, finnesh) off our village. In (menuts, minutes), the (disurt, desert) will begin to return and our land will be (vacant, vacint). If our trees are (stolin, stolen), our lives will also end!

FUN WITH WORDS Use Spelling Words to complete the sentences.

WELCOME, VISITORS!

You can't pick even one __14__ from our trees. (That's because those snacks grow underground!) But if you've __15__ to stay here for a while, our trees will shelter you. And if you choose to __16__ on, they'll give you fruits to take on your journey.

1. _____
2. _____
3. _____
4. _____
5. _____
6. _____

7. _____
8. _____
9. _____
10. _____
11. _____
12. _____
13. _____

14. _____
15. _____
16. _____

COAST TO COAST "The People Who Hugged the Trees" • Harcourt Brace School Publishers

Military
★ W O R D S ★

troop
fortress
soldier
officer

SPELLING LOG Think about how you might use these Military Words in your writing. Add them to your Spelling Log.

1. _____
2. _____
3. _____
4. _____
5. _____
6. _____
7. _____
8. _____
9. _____
10. _____

11. _____
12. _____
13. _____
14. _____
15. _____
16. _____

Vocabulary WordShop

In "The People Who Hugged the Trees," one woman named Amrita challenged a Maharajah's army in order to save her village. Now read this paragraph about a different kind of attack. For each icon, or picture, write the corresponding Military Word in the blank on the left. Use the plural form of a word if necessary.

soldier   troop   officer   fortress

Once upon a time, a 1 🏰 was attacked by the enemy. The

2 👥 had been sleeping and did not hear the approach of

enemy forces. But one 3 👤 was standing guard and saw the

enemy advance. He sounded the alarm, and soon there were many

4 👤👤 , 5 👥👥👥 , and 6 👤👤👤 at the walls

fighting to save their 7 🏰 . Eventually, the defending 8 👥

👥👥 won the battle, and the commanding 9 👤 awarded a

medal to the watchful 10 👤 who had sounded the alarm.

11–16. Now think of other words you might use to name military people or groups. Write them on the lines.

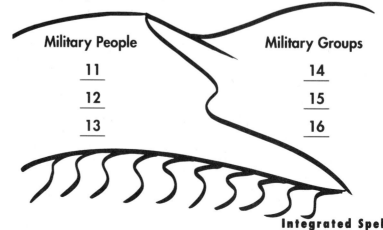

Military People	Military Groups
11	14
12	15
13	16

Name _____

WHAT'S IN A WORD?

Officer is based on the Latin word *officium*, which first meant "a helpful act or service, a kindness." Later the word came to mean "a duty or job." Now *officer* refers to someone in a position of authority or command, but not necessarily in the military.

1. Name another book with an officer as a character. Write the book's title, and describe the kind of authority the officer has.

1. _____

_____

_____

_____

_____

_____

SYNONYMS   Synonyms are words that have almost the same meanings. Find a word in each sentence that is a synonym for a word in the box. Underline the word in the sentence, and write its synonym on the correct line at the right.

> hurried   battered   ruled   defy   drifted

2. A Maharajah controlled India and wanted to cut down its trees.

3. But one woman decided to challenge the Maharajah's order.

4. The desert wind struck the small village.

5. The sand flowed over the roads and paths.

6. People rushed to the trees to protect them.

2. _____

3. _____

4. _____

5. _____

6. _____

ROUND ROBIN   Memorize as many Spelling Words as you can. Then sit with three classmates. One player writes a Spelling Word and passes the paper to the right. Each classmate adds a new Spelling Word. If a player can't think of a word, someone may give a clue. If the clue doesn't help, the person writes *blank*. Continue until all the words are listed.

1. quiet
2. liar
3. cruel
4. riot
5. giant
6. ruin
7. diet
8. poem
9. lion
10. prior
11. fuel
12. react
13. triumph
14. science
15. poet
16. create

Your Own
★ W O R D S ★

Look for other words spelled with the VV pattern, and add them to the lists. For example, you might find *dial* and *fluid* in an automobile manual.

17. _____
18. _____
19. _____
20. _____

Spelling Patterns: VV Words

Each Spelling Word has two vowels in the middle that are pronounced separately. As you pronounce each word, notice that it is divided into two syllables between the two vowel sounds.

Sort the Spelling Words in a way that will help you remember them. Four example words are given.

trial
_____
_____
_____
_____
_____
_____
_____
_____
_____

duet
_____
_____
_____
_____

neon
_____
_____

going
_____
_____
_____
_____

▶ When a word has two vowel sounds between two consonants, divide the word between the two vowel sounds. Then spell the word, one syllable at a time.

COAST TO COAST "The Third Planet" • Harcourt Brace School Publishers

Integrated Spelling

Name _____

Strategy Workshop

PROOFREADING: Adjoining Vowels A common error when writing a word that includes two adjoining vowels is to write the vowel letters in the wrong order. So when you are proofreading, pronounce words carefully. Listen for the sounds the letters spell, and be sure you have written the vowel letters in the correct order.

Pronounce the words below. Circle the misspelled words, and write the words in which the vowels appear in the correct order.

1. roit   riot   2. liar   laier
3. triumph   truimph 4. peom   poem
5. lion   loing   6. peot   poet

7–12. Government officials in rainforest countries might write a letter like this to farmers and ranchers. Study the word pairs in parentheses. Choose the correct spellings and write those words.

> Esteemed Farmers and Ranchers:
>   In (prior, proir) letters, we encouraged you to clear rainforest land for farming and (feul, fuel). Now, however, we must (raect, react) to a growing problem.
> Our (quiet, queit), valuable forest is disappearing! (Science, Sceince) has proved that clearing trees will (craete, create) areas where nothing will grow. Please stop cutting the trees.
>   Sincerely,
>   Secretary of Forestry

FUN WITH WORDS Write Spelling Words to replace 13–16.

You must go on a __13__, or you'll __14__ your health!

Don't be __15__! I just had a __16__ lunch!

1. _____
2. _____
3. _____
4. _____
5. _____
6. _____

7. _____
8. _____
9. _____
10. _____
11. _____
12. _____

13. _____
14. _____
15. _____
16. _____

grasslands
tundra
marshes
delta

SPELLING LOG Think about how you might use these Ecosystem Words in your writing. Then add them to your Spelling Log.

1. _____
2. _____
3. _____
4. _____

Vocabulary WordShop

Write the Ecosystem Words on the lines at the left.

1
2
3
4

5–12. Now think of other words related to ecosystems in our world. Write them on the lines at the left.

5. _____
6. _____
7. _____
8. _____
9. _____
10. _____
11. _____
12. _____

5
6
7
8
9
10

11
12

COAST TO COAST "The Third Planet" • Harcourt Brace School Publishers

Integrated Spelling

Name _____

WHAT'S IN A WORD?

Grasslands is a compound word first used in 1682. Not surprisingly, it describes land on which grass—and little else—grows.

1. Use the dictionary to find two more compound words or phrases that are made from *grass* or *land* and another word.

1. _____
   _____
   _____
   _____
   _____

COMPOUND WORDS Compound words are made of two or more words. Some are written as one word, as in *grasslands.* Others, like *grade school,* are two words. Still others are hyphenated, as in *self-confidence.* Complete these sentences using the words below.

----
     outline   year-round   bright-eyed   wildlife
----

2. The Earth's ___ lives in varied ecosystems.
3. When the water in a lake dries up, you can see the ___ of the water's usual level.
4. It rains ___ in tropical regions.
5. The animals in a healthy ecosystem are active and ___.

2. _____
3. _____
4. _____
5. _____

POEM PARTNERS With a partner, write some two-line rhymes. First, divide the Spelling Words into two groups. Each of you writes the first line of a rhyme for five of your Spelling Words. Try to end each first line with a sound that suggests a Spelling Word for a rhyme. For example, one of you might write "What a big dinner we ate . . ." which suggests the word *create* as a rhyme. Trade lists, and write the second line of your partner's rhymes, ending each one with a Spelling Word. Work together to write rhymes for the remaining words.

COAST TO COAST "The Third Planet" • Harcourt Brace School Publishers

Integrated Spelling

SPELLING ★ WORDS ★

1. _pioneer_
2. _driver_
3. _goalie_
4. _dentist_
5. _catcher_
6. _engineer_
7. _mayor_
8. _pianist_
9. _rookie_
10. _tourist_
11. _beggar_
12. _librarian_
13. _scientist_
14. _musician_
15. _director_
16. _burglar_

Your Own ★ W O R D S ★

Look for other words that name people to add to the list. You might find *vegetarian* in an article about food.

17. _____
18. _____
19. _____
20. _____

Words Like
pioneer **and** *tourist*

These Spelling Words name people in certain occupations. Each word was formed by adding a suffix to a base word.

Sort the Spelling Words in a way that will help you remember them. Five headings are given.

-eer

_____
_____
_____

-ie

_____
_____
_____

-ist

_____
_____
_____
_____

-ian

_____
_____
_____

-ar, -or, -er

_____
_____
_____
_____
_____
_____
_____

▶ The suffixes *-eer, -ie, -ist, -ian, -ar, -or,* and *-er* often mean "a person connected to a certain occupation" or "one who does" a particular job.

COAST TO COAST "Sugaring Time" and "To Space and Back" • Harcourt Brace School Publishers

Integrated Spelling

Strategy Workshop

SPELLING CLUES: Related Words The base
words used for the Spelling Words can also form other
related words.

Write the Spelling Word that is related to each of the
words below.

1. piano   2. musical
3. catch   4. goal
5. library   6. mayoral

7–12. Below is an essay on collecting maple sap at sugaring
time. Change each base word in parentheses into a related
Spelling Word. Write the correct spellings.

> No one can stand around and be a (tour) at
> sugaring time. Everyone has a job. Mom is the
> (drive), guiding the horses through the snow to the
> maple trees. Dad is a (science), testing the temperature
> of the boiling sap. An (engine) must have designed
> our sugarhouse so gravity would help the syrup flow
> downhill. I have watched sugaring so many times
> that I could be the (direct) in a year or two.
>   Our (dental) tells us not to taste so much syrup,
> but we can't help ourselves. Sugaring time comes
> only once a year!

1. _____
2. _____
3. _____
4. _____
5. _____
6. _____

7. _____
8. _____
9. _____
10. _____
11. _____
12. _____

WORKING WITH MEANING Use the Spelling Words
to answer these two riddles.

What is the difference between
a pioneer and a rookie?

A 13 is a person in a new place,
but a 14 is a person in a new job.

What is the difference between a burglar and
a beggar?

A 15 asks before taking, but a 16
takes without asking.

13. _____
14. _____
15. _____
16. _____

Scenic ★ WORDS ★

landscape
scenery
panorama
vista

SPELLING LOG Think about how you might use these Scenic Words in your writing. Add them to your Spelling Log.

1. _____
   _____
2. _____
3. _____
   _____
4. _____
   _____

5. _____
6. _____
7. _____
8. _____

Vocabulary WordShop

Imagine you're an astronaut aboard a space shuttle during launch. Fill in the Scenic Words to describe what you can see around you.

The Scenic Words include two pairs of words that are almost synonyms. In some sentences, either word in the pair would be correct. Check a dictionary if you wish.

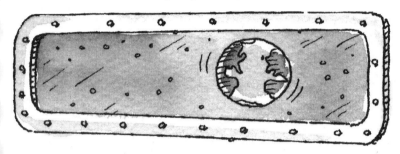

This is unbelievable! As the shuttle moves higher, I can no longer see smaller parts of the __1__, such as lakes and cities. However, I can still see larger objects in a __2__, such as mountain ranges. At this height, I can see almost the entire __3__ of our nation from coast to coast. A few minutes ago, I could see from Florida to New York. My __4__ now includes the area from Los Angeles north to Oregon.

5–8. Now think of other words you might use to name places you see. Write them on the lines at the left.

COAST TO COAST "Sugaring Time" and "To Space and Back" • Harcourt Brace School Publishers

Name _____

WHAT'S IN A WORD?

The word *panorama* comes from two Greek words, *pan*, "all," and *horama*, "a view." More than 200 years ago, *panorama* was the name of a special device that could show viewers an entire landscape, one section at a time. The picture actually unrolled! Now *panorama* means "a complete view in every direction."

1. Write a sentence including the word *panorama* to describe what you can see from the front door of the house or building where you live.

1. _____
_____
_____
_____
_____

NEW MEANINGS FOR OLD As technology changes, so does our language. The space program has given us many new words and a number of new meanings for old words. Write the correct words on the lines. Use a dictionary if you need help.

----
    hatch   liftoff   air lock   reentry
----

2. Astronauts empty the air from the ___, so that the atmosphere there is equal to that in space.
3. One very dangerous time is___, because the shuttle carries thousands of pounds of explosive fuel.
4. Tiles protect the outside of the shuttle from the heat during___.
5. If the___doesn't close tightly, the shuttle may leak oxygen into space.

2. _____
3. _____
4. _____
5. _____

SILENT SPELLING Divide the Spelling Words so you and a partner each have eight words. Take turns pantomiming the actions of the person named by your Spelling Word. The other player tries to guess the occupation and writes the Spelling Word. Continue taking turns until you have spelled all the words correctly.

Name _____

Practice Test

A. Read each phrase. On the answer sheet, mark the letter of the correctly spelled word.

Example: a fast game of _____

A tennes   B tinnis   C tenis   D tennis

1. an _____ in my allowance
- A increese
- B increase
- C inkrease
- D inkreaze

2. a _____ in the tree
- A robin
- B robbin
- C roben
- D rabin

3. a _____ on a baseball team
- A cather
- B cachor
- C catcher
- D catchar

4. study _____ in a laboratory
- A science
- B sciens
- C sceince
- D scince

5. _____ the flood
- A cervive
- B servive
- C sorvive
- D survive

6. a flattering _____
- A portriat
- B purtrat
- C portrait
- D purtrit

7. time to _____
- A finich
- B finish
- C finishe
- D finesh

8. a concert _____
- A piannist
- B painist
- C pienist
- D pianist

9. an ancient _____
- A riun
- B ruin
- C ruen
- D ruan

10. a _____ on a hockey team
- A goalie
- B goley
- C golie
- D goly

EXAMPLE			
A	B	C	**D**

ANSWERS			
1. A	B	C	D
2. A	B	C	D
3. A	B	C	D
4. A	B	C	D
5. A	B	C	D
6. A	B	C	D
7. A	B	C	D
8. A	B	C	D
9. A	B	C	D
10. A	B	C	D

COAST TO COAST Unit 5 Review • Harcourt Brace School Publishers

Name _____

B. On the answer sheet, mark the letter of the underlined word that is misspelled in each sentence.

Example: I saw a <u>panthur</u> at the <u>circus</u>.
           A   B

1. The <u>libarian</u> read his favorite <u>poem</u>.
        A   B

2. The <u>pioneer</u> crossed the hot, dry <u>dessert</u>.
       A   B

3. I walked through the <u>quiet</u> <u>orcherd</u>.
                        A   B

4. Two <u>members</u> of the group came <u>foreward</u>.
       A   B

5. The <u>turist</u> wanted to <u>purchase</u> a map.
       A   B

6. My <u>dentist</u> says,"Eat fruit <u>insted</u> of candy."
      A   B

7. He smiled in his <u>momemt</u> of <u>triumph</u>.
                    A   B

8. I will <u>creeate</u> a <u>giant</u> mural.
          A   B

9. We met in a <u>pirvate</u> <u>office</u>.
               A   B

10. <u>Althogh</u> I left early, I was still ten <u>minutes</u> late.
    A   B

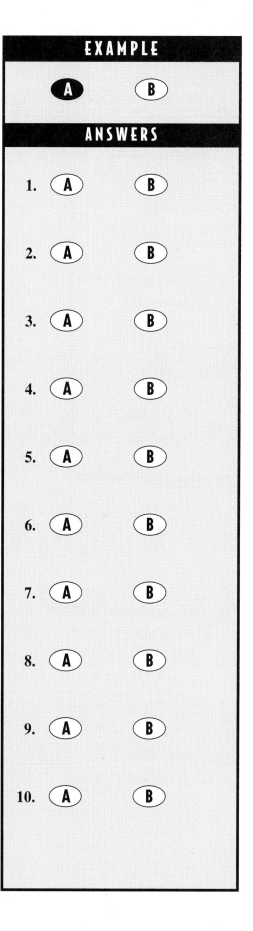

Unit 5: Writing Activities

WORDS TO WATCH FOR

laugh
upon
everything
someone
strange
we're
their
it's
national
period

The Planet and I

You probably spend a lot of time with people, but how much contact do you have with other creatures on our "planet of life"? Describe some interactions you have with Earth's plants and animals. Be specific and use vivid words. For example, instead of writing "I see a stray dog sometimes," you might write this: "Yesterday I watched a little spotted dog with drooping ears and hungry eyes follow people up and down the sidewalk." Use sensory words to help readers see and feel what you see and feel. As you write, use as many Words to Watch For as you can.

Tips for Spelling Success

When proofreading, check the spelling of troublesome words, especially those with two vowels next to each other, like *react* and *although*. If you're not sure of the spelling, check a dictionary.

To Hug or Not to Hug

Tips for Spelling Success

- When you spell a compound word, look for the little words in the longer word.

- If the little words are spelled correctly, the compound word should also be correct.

- Remember that some compounds are spelled as one word; some have a hyphen; and some are spelled as two words!

Amrita and the villagers hugged their trees long ago to keep them safe. Should people still hug them? Is it more important today to preserve our forests or to preserve people's jobs as loggers and builders? Read a few magazine or newspaper articles about the subject, and make some notes on index cards. Then work with your classmates. Divide a bulletin board into two sections. On one side, place the index cards of students who want to preserve the trees. On the other side, place the cards of students who want to preserve jobs. Be sure each student submits a card.

COAST TO COAST Unit 5 Review • Harcourt Brace School Publishers

Trees and the Environment

After reading about the importance of trees in the environment, think again about the importance of preserving our forests. Then write two paragraphs on the subject. In the first paragraph, explain what happens to the land when trees are cut down. In the second paragraph, explain how trees protect the environment.

Arrange your paragraphs as follows. Write one fact followed by one example or piece of evidence to support it. Then write your next fact and next example, and so on. Do the same in the second paragraph. Link your sentences with words of comparison or contrast.

Tips for Spelling Success

Expressions of comparison include *likewise, in addition,* and *in the same way.* Those showing contrast include *on the other hand, however,* and *in contrast.* Spell compounds such as *likewise* and *moreover* as one word.

Space to Earth

Imagine that you are in a space shuttle flying miles above Earth. For some reason your messages to Mission Control are not being sent properly, and some words have only consonants. Write a few messages in which one or two words per sentence have only consonants. Exchange messages with a partner, and decipher each other's words. Here are some examples:

"With people floating, it's like a crcs up here!" (*circus*)

"We will trmph! Each one of us is a pnr!" (*triumph, pioneer*)

"It's just that we don't trvl in a covered wagon." (*travel*)

Tips for Spelling Success

Choose words from the last five lessons that work with a space topic. Since words with two vowels together can be tricky, review the suggestions offered in Lesson 28 beginning on page 118.

Name _____

Compound Words

A compound word is formed by joining two smaller words. Some compounds, like *fireplace,* are spelled with the two words joined together. Others, such as *seventy-five,* are spelled with a hyphen between the two words.

Sort the Spelling Words in a way that will help you remember them. Two example words are given.

SPELLING
★ WORDS ★

1. *fireplace*
2. *brand-new*
3. *upstairs*
4. *doorway*
5. *backyard*
6. *flashlight*
7. *everybody*
8. *background*
9. *outdoors*
10. *make-believe*
11. *farmland*
12. *lifeguard*
13. *Thanksgiving*
14. *earthquake*
15. *rattlesnake*
16. *seventy-five*

Your Own
★ WORDS ★

Look for other compound words to add to the lists. For example, you might find *keyboard* and *network* in an article about computers.

17. _____
18. _____
19. _____
20. _____

songbook

bushy-tailed

▶ A compound word is made up of two smaller words.
▶ Some compound words are written as one word. Others are hyphenated.

Strategy Workshop

SPELLING CLUES: Smaller Words When you spell a compound word, identify the two small words from which it is made. If you're not sure how to join the words, check a dictionary.

Choose words from the box to complete six Spelling Words.

back	Thanks	quake	land	life	believe

1. earth
2. guard
3. yard
4. giving
5. make
6. farm

7–12. Read this letter that a Spanish settler might have written. Complete each Spelling Word by adding another word to the word in parentheses. Write the Spelling Words.

Dear Pedro,

(body) misses you very much. Every morning I stand in our (way) and watch for you. We have (brand) twin goats that you would like very much. Yesterday I saw a (rattle) that was six feet long! In (five) days it will be my birthday. I wish you could be here then. Mamá lights a fire in the (fire) every night to help you find your way home.

Until then,
Miguel

FUN WITH WORDS Write the four Spelling Words that match the shapes below. Note the difference between a tall letter and a letter in which a part goes below the writing line.

13.
14.
15.
16.

1. _____
2. _____
3. _____
4. _____
5. _____
6. _____

7. _____
8. _____
9. _____
10. _____
11. _____
12. _____

13. _____
14. _____
15. _____
16. _____

COAST TO COAST "Spanish Pioneers of the Southwest" • Harcourt Brace School Publishers

Vocabulary WordShop

Imagine that you're Pedro, the older brother in "Spanish Pioneers of the Souhwest." You have been kidnapped by Navajos but are not in danger. Use Souhwestern Spanish words in your letter to your younger brother Miguel. Write one of your Southwestern Spanish Words as a plural.

Dear Miguel,

　　I miss you and our family, but I am well. I wish I were living in our __1__, but I also like the hills where I live now. Like our people, the Navajos have many happy celebrations. And even though they prefer quiet ceremonies to noisy __2__, both groups have good things to eat afterward.

　　I am treated well and even have my own pony. Do you still have our __3__ Gaspar? Someday I hope to be back in our warm __4__, eating chili stew with you and the family.

　　　　　　　　　Until then,

　　　　　　　　　Pedro

5–8. Think of other Spanish words that are now part of the English language. Write the words. Check their spellings.

5. _____

6. _____

7. _____

8. _____

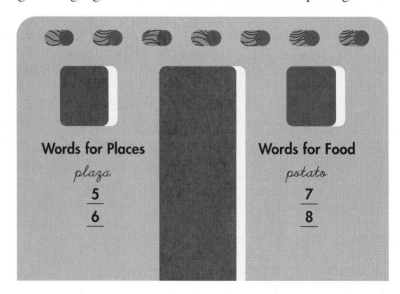

Words for Places

plaza

__5__

__6__

Words for Food

potato

__7__

__8__

COAST TO COAST "Spanish Pioneers of the Southwest" • Harcourt Brace School Publishers

Name _____

What do a horse and a dove have in common? In Spanish, the word *palomino* means "like a dove." When we borrowed this word, we used it to describe a light tan horse, as the Spaniards did. But unless English-speaking people knew Spanish, they wouldn't understand what the horse and the dove have in common. It seems that palominos and doves are the same color!

1. In English, the word *burrow* is pronounced like the word *burro*. Yes, they are homophones. But check a dictionary to learn whether they mean the same thing. Then write a sentence for each word.

MORE BORROWED SPANISH Match each word

from Spanish with its definition. Write the correct answers.

2. a blanketlike cape   siesta

3. an afternoon nap   adobe

4. sun-dried bricks made of clay and straw   mesa

5. an area of high, flat land   poncho

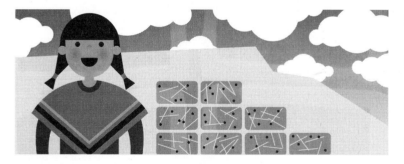

1. _____
_____
_____
_____
_____
_____
_____
_____
_____
_____
_____

2. _____
3. _____
4. _____
5. _____

COMPOUND CONCENTRATION Work with a

partner to write on separate cards the individual words that make up each compound Spelling Word. Turn the cards face down, and use them to play Concentration. Each partner turns over a pair of cards. If they form a Spelling Word, and if the player can spell the word without looking at the cards, he or she can keep them and take another turn. The player with more cards at the end of the game wins.

SPELLING ★ WORDS ★

1. wisdom
2. divide
3. division
4. wise
5. unity
6. athlete
7. reception
8. popular
9. receive
10. athletic
11. united
12. population
13. application
14. compete
15. apply
16. competitive

Your Own ★ WORDS ★

Look for other pairs of related words to add to the lists. *Define* and *definition* are in any dictionary.

17. _____
18. _____
19. _____
20. _____

Related Words

This list contains eight pairs of related Spelling Words—either a base word and a form related to it, or two forms related to the same base word. Notice how the spelling and pronunciation of the base word change when a related word is formed.

Sort the Spelling Words into their related pairs.

▶ The spelling and pronunciation of a base word often change when a related word is formed.

▶ For base words ending in *e,* a long vowel often becomes short in the related word.

COAST TO COAST "Children of the Wild West" • Harcourt Brace School Publishers

Name _____

Strategy Workshop

PROOFREADING: Related Words Check your
spelling of all words related to a base word. Be sure to make
necessary changes in the base word before you add a suffix.

For each Spelling Word listed below, write the related
Spelling Word.

1. athlete   2. compete
3. population   4. united
5. receive

1. _____

2. _____

3. _____

4. _____

5. _____

6–12. Study this letter from a young teacher. For each word in
parentheses, write the correct related Spelling Word.

> To the (popular) of Sunny Valley;
>   Please accept my (apply) to teach in your town.
> I am only sixteen, but my skills can (competitive)
> with those of older teachers. I can teach spelling,
> multiplication, and (divide). Your children will
> (reception) my full attention.
>   I hope you are all (unity) in a wish to hire me.
> Looking forward to a reply, I await your (wisdom)
> decision.
>   Miss Letitia Swinson

6. _____

7. _____

8. _____

9. _____

10. _____

11. _____

12. _____

FUN WITH WORDS Use Spelling Words to replace
13–16 and complete the poem.

I decided to __13__,

And I will tell you why.

I have __14__ to share.

I can teach anywhere.

Although I'm not an __15__,

My teaching skills are complete.

It is my greatest pride

To teach children to __16__.

13. _____

14. _____

15. _____

16. _____

settlers

cabins

wilderness

frontier

SPELLING LOG Think about how you might use these Western Movement Words in your writing. Add them to your Spelling Log.

1. _____
2. _____
3. _____
4. _____

Vocabulary WordShop

In "Children of the Wild West," Russell Freedman describes the hardships that families faced on the frontier. Imagine that you've recently arrived there and are writing to a friend back home. Use Western Movement Words to complete this letter.

Dear Julia,
We have finally reached the West and are living in a <u>1</u> settlement. Traveling in covered wagons with other hopeful <u>2</u> was hard. But now that we have built <u>3</u>, our lives are easier. Still we are in the <u>4</u>, and the woods are full of bears! Father wants to move closer to the ocean, so I suppose we are not truly "at home" yet.

Your friend,

5–8. Now think of other words you might use in writing about the western frontier. Write them on the lines at the left.

<u>5</u>
<u>6</u>
<u>7</u>
<u>8</u>

5. _____
6. _____
7. _____
8. _____

Integrated Spelling

Name _____

WHAT'S IN A WORD?

In frontier days, teachers received low wages because the towns that paid them often had little money. To make up for this, teachers lived with the families of their students and were given room and board. The phrase *room and board* simply means "a place to sleep and food to eat." The word *board* comes from its original meaning, "table," a place where food is served.

1. Write what you think a *boarder* is. Then check a dictionary for the meaning, and make any changes needed in your definition.

1. _____
_____
_____
_____
_____
_____
_____
_____

DICTIONARY SKILLS A dictionary can help you with the spellings of plural words. First, look up the singular form of the word. If a plural form is not listed, just add *s* to make it plural. If a plural word is given, that is the form to use. Try it yourself. Write the plural forms of these words. Check a dictionary to see whether you're right.

> **cal·en·dar** [kal′ən·dər] *n.* **1** An arrangement of time into years, months, weeks, and days. **2** A table showing the days, weeks, months of a year. **3** A schedule or list of events or appointments: a social *calendar.*
> **calf** [kaf] *n., pl.* **calves** [kavz] **1** The young of the cow or bovine animals. **2** The young of some other mammals, as the seal or whale. **3** Calfskin

2. class	3. family	4. copy
5. child	6. almanac	7. youngster
8. emergency	9. encyclopedia	

2. _____
3. _____
4. _____
5. _____
6. _____
7. _____
8. _____
9. _____

MISSING RELATIVES Divide the Spelling Words so you and a partner each have eight. For each of your words, write a sentence that includes one Spelling Word but has a blank for the related Spelling Word. If you received both related words in a pair, write a sentence for each one. Then exchange papers and fill in each other's related Spelling Words.

1. *half*
2. *island*
3. *answer*
4. *palm*
5. *wreck*
6. *wrap*
7. *gnaw*
8. *would*
9. *sword*
10. *aisle*
11. *hymn*
12. *reign*
13. *column*
14. *yolk*
15. *gnome*
16. *wrinkled*

Your Own
★ W O R D S ★

Look for other words with "silent" letters to add to the lists. For example, you might find *sign* and *writing* in a book about sign language.

17. _____
18. _____
19. _____
20. _____

Words with "Silent" Letters

Each Spelling Word includes a consonant that is not pronounced. These "silent" letters can make words harder to spell. Say each word aloud, and notice which consonant is not pronounced.

Sort the Spelling Words in a way that will help you remember them.

"silent" g

"silent" s

"silent" n

"silent" l

"silent" w

▶ "Silent" letters are often found in these consonant pairs: *s(sl)*; *g(gn)*; *l(lm, lf, ld, lk)*; *n(mn)*; *w(wr, sw)*.

Strategy Workshop

PROOFREADING: Missing Letters It's easy to omit the "silent" letters in the Spelling Words. Proofread carefully to make sure you've included them.

Put a caret (^) in each word below to show where a "silent" letter has been omitted. Write the words correctly.

1. i l a n d   2. h a f   3. c o l u m
4. s o r d   5. r i n k l e d   6. a n s e r

7–12. Some Spelling Words are homophones of other words. They sound alike but have different spellings and meanings. Read these rules posted in a train. Write each Spelling Word that sounds like its homophone in parentheses. Be sure to include the "silent" letters.

1. _____
2. _____
3. _____
4. _____
5. _____
6. _____

Rules for Behavior

7. Do not stand in the (I'll).
8. (Rap) up your crumbs so they won't attract ants.
9. We (wood) appreciate your being quiet.
10. Let peace (rain).
11. At breakfast, do not complain if your egg (yoke) is broken.
12. At night, listen quietly if someone sings a (him).

7. _____
8. _____
9. _____
10. _____
11. _____
12. _____

FUN WITH WORDS Write Spelling Words for each rhyming riddle.

What is a toadstool?	a home for a _13_
What is a still hand?	a calm _14_
What's an accident on a nature trail?	a trek _15_
What's a rule for eating a drumstick?	a _16_ law

13. _____
14. _____
15. _____
16. _____

Railroad
★ WORDS ★

conductor
passengers
railroad
porter

SPELLING LOG Think about how you might use these Railroad Words in your writing. Add them to your Spelling Log.

1. _____

2. _____

3. _____

4. _____

5. _____

6. _____

7. _____

8. _____

9. _____

_____

_____

_____

_____

_____

_____

_____

Vocabulary WordShop

In "A Family Apart," the Kelly children travel by train to Missouri. Imagine that you're one of them, writing to a relative in Albany. Use Railroad Words to complete your letter.

Dear Aunt Helen,
  I miss you, but I'm trying to learn as much as I can during my __1__ trip. I already know that the __2__ is the person who checks our tickets, and the __3__ is the one who carries suitcases. Only the adult __4__ have suitcases, but he'd carry mine too, if I had one. Please come and visit me in Missouri.

5–8. Now think of other words you might use to tell about a train trip. Write them on the lines.

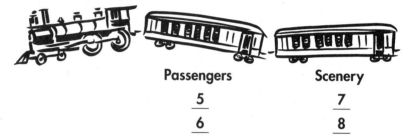

Passengers	Scenery
5	7
6	8

WHAT'S IN A WORD?

Hannibal, Missouri, was named after a creek that ran through the city early in its history. And even earlier, Hannibal Creek had been named for the great leader Hannibal. Hannibal was the fierce commander of an army from Carthage, Africa, during a series of three wars with Rome. He is probably most famous for daring to drive battle elephants across the Alps and using them to fight against the Roman legions.

9. Find out how another place was named. The place name may be from another language, such as *Los Angeles*, which comes from Spanish. Or maybe it was named for a person. Houston, Texas, for example, was named for General Sam Houston, who later became president of the Republic of Texas. Write what you learn, and share it with the class.

COAST TO COAST "A Family Apart" • Harcourt Brace School Publishers

Name _____

MULTIPLE MEANINGS Some of the Spelling Words
are homophones, which sound alike but have different meanings
and spellings. Other pairs of words are homographs. They have
the same spellings and pronunciations, but different meanings.
For example, *bow,* meaning "a tied ribbon," and *bow,* meaning
"a tool used to shoot an arrow," are homographs.

Complete each sentence below with a word from the box. You
will use each word in two sentences to show two meanings of the
word. Use a dictionary if you wish.

```
        train      kind      board      bills
```

Someone carried a money clip that held dollar 1 .

The children got on 2 the train.

Frances hoped their new parents
would be 3 to them.

She tried to 4 the children to
be polite.

The 5 trip lasted for several days.

What 6 of place would they be
living in?

A 7 in the floor of the train was
loose.

Mrs. Kelly couldn't pay her 8 ,
so she was forced to put the
children up for adoption.

1. _____
2. _____
3. _____
4. _____
5. _____
6. _____
7. _____
8. _____

SILENT SCRAMBLE Divide the Spelling Words so you
and a partner each have eight. Mix up the letters of each word so
that they're out of order. Then exchange lists. Each of you must
try to put your partner's scrambled letters back in order to form
Spelling Words. Check each other's spelling, and take additional
time to practice any words you spelled incorrectly.

Places and People

COAST TO COAST "Hector Lives in the United States Now" • Harcourt Brace School Publishers

SPELLING
★ WORDS ★

1. Japan
2. American
3. America
4. Japanese
5. African
6. English
7. Mexico
8. Asia
9. Mexican
10. Africa
11. Asian
12. England
13. Vietnamese
14. Greek
15. Greece
16. Vietnam

Your Own
★ ★ WORDS ★

Look for other words that name people and places, and add them to the lists. You might find *Canada* and *Canadian* in an article about the *Inuit* people.

17. _____
18. _____
19. _____
20. _____

Some of the Spelling Words name places. The others name people or languages from those places, and can also be used as describing words. Notice how each place name is changed to form the related word.

Sort the Spelling Words in a way that will help you remember them. Two example words are given.

France	French

▶ Names of nations and continents are proper nouns. They and their related words are always capitalized.

▶ Suffixes added to place names to form related words include *-ese*, *-ish*, and *-an*. Some place names, such as *Greece,* change in other ways.

Integrated Spelling

Strategy Workshop

DICTIONARY: Using a Pronunciation Key

When the name of a place is changed to the name of the people who live there, the pronunciation of the word also changes. A dictionary can help you say both words correctly.

GUIDE WORDS The guide words at the top of each Spelling Dictionary page show you the first and last entry words on that page. Look at the guide words to see if the word you want can be found on that page. Use the guide words below. Locate the Spelling Words that refer to people living in a certain place. Write the Spelling Words that name these people.

1. apartment—brief   2. acrobat—any way

3. earnings—farther   4. fuel—hospital

5–12. Each entry word in the dictionary is followed by its pronunciation. Accent marks (′ and ′) show which syllable or syllables are accented. For the word *Norway,* the pronunciation looks like this: [nôr′wā]. The first syllable of *Norway* is accented.

Write the correct spelling for each pronunciation. Then underline the syllable with the heaviest accent. Use the Pronunciation Key in your Spelling Dictionary if you need help.

5. [mek′sə·kō]   6. [mek′sə·kən]

7. [jə·pan′]   8. [jap′ə·nēz′]

9. [af′ri·kə]   10. [af′ri·kən]

11. [vē′et·näm′]   12. [vē·et′nə·mēz′]

WORKING WITH MEANING Use Spelling Words to answer these geography questions.

13. Which continent includes China and India?

14. What word is in the names of two continents?

15. Which nation is south of Scotland?

16. Which nation borders the Aegean Sea?

1. _____

2. _____

3. _____

4. _____

5. _____

6. _____

7. _____

8. _____

9. _____

10. _____

11. _____

12. _____

13. _____

14. _____

15. _____

16. _____

COAST TO COAST "Hector Lives in the United States Now" • Harcourt Brace School Publishers

Location ★ WORDS ★

neighborhood
apartment
alley
vicinity

SPELLING LOG Think about how you might use these Location Words in your writing. Add them to your Spelling Log.

1._____
2._____
3._____
4._____

Vocabulary WordShop

In Joan Hewett's "Hector Lives in the United States Now," Hector is a Mexican American boy who describes his school and friends. Use the Location Words to complete a letter that Hector might have written to his grandmother.

Dear Grandma,

*How are you? Someday I hope you will be able to see the homes in our **1**. We live in an **2** in a big building near a bakery, my school, and our church. My friends and I like to play soccer in the **3** that separates two of the buildings. I know it's a long trip to Los Angeles, but if you are ever in our **4**, please come to stay with us for a while.*

Your grandson,
Hector

5–8. Hector lives in the city. Now think of two words you might use in describing each of these other places. Write your words on the lines.

5._____
6._____
7._____
8._____

COAST TO COAST "Hector Lives in the United States Now" • Harcourt Brace School Publishers

WHAT'S IN A WORD?

Neighborhood is based on two Old English words: *neah*, which means "near," and *gebur*, meaning "dweller." So a *neighbor* is someone who dwells, or lives, nearby.

1. Write a sentence using the word *neighborhood* to compare the setting of "Hector Lives in the United States Now" with the setting of another book you have read.

ANTONYMS Antonyms are pairs of words that mean the opposite of each other, such as *hot* and *cold*. Read sentences 2–5, and find antonyms in the box to replace the words in parentheses. Write each antonym.

familiar   annoyed   aloud   prosperous

2. Hector and the other students read their reports (silently).
3. Hector's mother was (pleased) when he and his brother spoke quickly.
4. Their neighborhood looked very (strange) to Hector.
5. The Los Angeles area was more (poor) than the city Hector's family had left in Mexico.

1. _____
_____
_____
_____
_____
_____
_____
_____
_____

2. _____
3. _____
4. _____
5. _____

WORLDWIDE SPELLING Divide the Spelling Words so you and a partner each have the names of four nations or continents. Find a world map or a globe to share. Then locate each of the nations or continents named in your Spelling Words. Take turns pointing to a place on the globe and asking your partner to spell the name of the nation or continent and the name of the people who live there. Check each other's spelling and geography skills.

SPELLING
★ WORDS ★

1. *hospital*
2. *favorite*
3. *magazine*
4. *dinosaur*
5. *acrobat*
6. *volcano*
7. *recycle*
8. *energy*
9. *example*
10. *century*
11. *difficult*
12. *however*
13. *substitute*
14. *probably*
15. *library*
16. *suddenly*

Your Own
★ WORDS ★

Look for other three-syllable words to add to the lists. You might find *summary* and *impression* in a book review.

17. _____
18. _____
19. _____
20. _____

Words with Three Syllables

Each Spelling Word has three syllables, and each syllable has one vowel sound. In some words, the first syllable is accented. In others, the second syllable is emphasized.

Sort the Spelling Words in a way that will help you remember them. Two example words are given.

hurricane
_____
_____
_____
_____
_____
_____
_____
_____
_____
_____

determine
_____
_____
_____
_____

▶ When spelling a three-syllable word, listen to the vowel sound in each syllable. Then spell the word, one syllable at a time.

COAST TO COAST "The Green Book" and "Sarah, Plain and Tall" • Harcourt Brace School Publishers

Integrated Spelling

Name _____

Strategy Workshop

SPELLING CLUES: Writing Aloud When you're not sure how to spell a word, try saying the word aloud. Listen to the sounds you hear, and think about the letters that usually spell those sounds.

Read these word pairs aloud. Circle the misspelled words. Write the correct spelling for each word.

1. hospital   hopital   2. deenosaur   dinosaur
3. volcono   volcano   4. libary   library
5. magazine   magasyne   6. acrobat   acrobait

7–12. This paragraph might be the beginning of a story written by Pattie, the youngest child in "The Green Book." To help her write the paragraph, underline the words in parentheses that are spelled correctly. Write the words on the lines.

> We are (sudenly, suddenly) in a whole new world. At our settlement we must (recycle, resycle) everything and watch our food supply carefully. Many crops won't grow here. For (exsample, example), we must find other food to (substitute, subsitute) for lettuce and carrots. (Howevver, However), our wheat is doing well. I think we will be able to live here for a (sentury, century) or more!

WORKING WITH MEANING Use Spelling Words to replace 13–16 in this dialogue taking place on a strange world where moths talk and people don't.

That little one is my __13__. It would not be __14__ to catch him and put him in a jar.

Catching him __15__ is a lot of work. I don't have that much __16__ right now. Let's just watch him.

1. _____
2. _____
3. _____
4. _____
5. _____
6. _____

7. _____
8. _____
9. _____
10. _____
11. _____
12. _____

13. _____
14. _____
15. _____
16. _____

Movement
★ WORDS ★

mobile

traveler

transport

relocate

SPELLING LOG Think about how you might use these Movement Words in your writing. Add them to your Spelling Log.

1. _____
2. _____
3. _____
4. _____

Vocabulary WordShop

The paragraph below is part of a letter. In "Sarah, Plain and Tall," Sarah writes to Jacob and his children before she ever sees them. Use Movement Words to complete the letter.

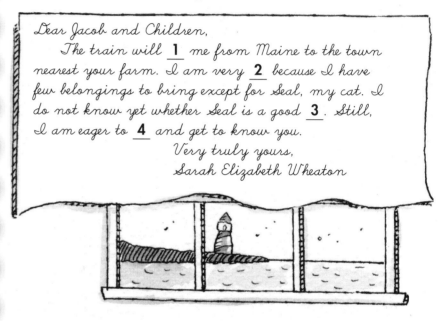

Dear Jacob and Children,

The train will __1__ me from Maine to the town nearest your farm. I am very __2__ because I have few belongings to bring except for Seal, my cat. I do not know yet whether Seal is a good __3__. Still, I am eager to __4__ and get to know you.

Very truly yours,

Sarah Elizabeth Wheaton

5–12. Now think of other words to describe movement from one place to another. Consider the kinds of travel popular in the past. Then think of words we'd use today—and in the future.

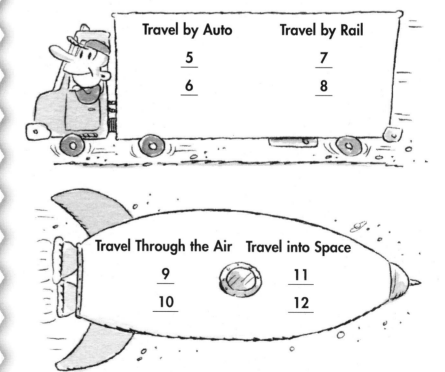

Travel by Auto	Travel by Rail
5	7
6	8

Travel Through the Air	Travel into Space
9	11
10	12

5. _____
6. _____
7. _____
8. _____
9. _____
10. _____
11. _____
12. _____

COAST TO COAST "The Green Book" and "Sarah, Plain and Tall" • Harcourt Brace School Publishers

Name _____

WHAT'S IN A WORD?

In England during the Middle Ages, most travelers walked over uneven paths through the forests. Journeys were so difficult that the English word *travel* came from the Old French word *travaillier*, which meant "to torture, torment, trouble." Later, *travaillier* also meant "to tire out by a journey."

But when the French settled in England during the eleventh century, *travaillier* became two separate English words. *Travel* simply means "journey." But *travail*, hinting at its French roots, means "pain and suffering."

1. List the titles and authors of two other selections based on travel or relocating. Explain the kinds of travel involved.

ANALOGIES In an analogy two pairs of words, though unlike, are similar in one striking way. Study this example:

STOP is to GO as HOT is to COLD.

How are *stop* and *go* similar to *hot* and *cold*? They are antonyms, or opposites! Whenever you see an analogy, you are asked to figure out how the word pairs are related.

Complete each analogy with a Movement Word.

| TRANSPORT | MOBILE | TRAVELER | RELOCATE |
---

2. SEA is to OCEAN as TOURIST is to ? .
3. RECEIVE is to ACCEPT as CARRY is to ? .
4. DAY is to NIGHT as UNMOVABLE is to ? .
5. TALK is to SPEAK as MOVE TO A NEW PLACE is to ? .

1. _____
_____
_____
_____
_____
_____
_____
_____
_____
_____
_____

2. _____
3. _____
4. _____
5. _____

TRIPLE CUT-UPS Working with a partner, write each Spelling Word on an index card. Then cut each card into three pieces, separating the syllables. Place them upside down and mix them up. Each player takes half the pieces and makes as many Spelling Words as possible. Then put the leftover pieces in a pile and construct the remaining Spelling Words.

Practice Test

A. Read each group of words. Find the underlined word that is misspelled. On the answer sheet, mark the letter of that word.

Example: A desert <u>island</u>   B African <u>design</u>
C go <u>upstares</u>   D a good <u>example</u>

EXAMPLE
Ⓐ   Ⓑ   ● Ⓒ   Ⓓ

1. A a long <u>aisle</u>   B short <u>divsion</u>
C <u>Greek</u> food   D <u>probably</u> gone

2. A <u>competative</u> team   B car <u>wreck</u>
C product of <u>Japan</u>   D complete <u>unity</u>

3. A egg <u>yolk</u>   B <u>Thankgiving</u> Day
C she <u>would</u> be there   D trip to <u>Asia</u>

4. A an old <u>hymn</u>   B <u>United</u> States
C <u>recycle</u> cans   D <u>rinkled</u> shirt

5. A <u>Vietnemese</u> people   B movie <u>magazine</u>
C dim <u>flashlight</u>   D <u>suddenly</u> dark

6. A <u>apply</u> for the job   B correct <u>answer</u>
C trained <u>lifeguard</u>   D <u>libary</u> book

7. A <u>seventy-five</u> cents   B <u>divide</u> in two
C daring <u>acrobat</u>   D <u>Enlish</u> accent

8. A <u>recieve</u> a package   B king's <u>reign</u>
C colored <u>background</u>   D full of <u>energy</u>

9. A strong <u>earthquake</u>   B a single <u>column</u>
C <u>populer</u> song   D <u>Mexican</u> city

10. A shores of <u>America</u>   B <u>atheletic</u> person
C wise <u>choice</u>   D great <u>outdoors</u>

ANSWERS
1. Ⓐ Ⓑ Ⓒ Ⓓ
2. Ⓐ Ⓑ Ⓒ Ⓓ
3. Ⓐ Ⓑ Ⓒ Ⓓ
4. Ⓐ Ⓑ Ⓒ Ⓓ
5. Ⓐ Ⓑ Ⓒ Ⓓ
6. Ⓐ Ⓑ Ⓒ Ⓓ
7. Ⓐ Ⓑ Ⓒ Ⓓ
8. Ⓐ Ⓑ Ⓒ Ⓓ
9. Ⓐ Ⓑ Ⓒ Ⓓ
10. Ⓐ Ⓑ Ⓒ Ⓓ

B. Each underlined word is misspelled. On the answer sheet, mark the letter of the correct spelling.

Many Amercan pioneers traveled west during the
     1
nineteenth sentury. California, with its rich framland,
          2   3
was a faverite destination. Some of the pioneers came
      4
from Englund and other European countries. Evrybody
     5   6
dreamed of a bran-new life. The popilation grew as
             7   8
more and more people made the diffacult journey.
                              9
Even the chance of a rattelsnake bite did not stop them.
                   10

1. A Ammerican   B American
     C Amerikan   D Ameracan

2. A century   B centurie
     C cenchury   D centery

3. A farm-land   B farmlande
     C farmland   D fahrmland

4. A favorete   B favorit
     C favurite   D favorite

5. A Englind   B England
     C Ingland   D Englend

6. A Everybodie   B Everybody
     C Everybudy   D Everrybody

7. A brand-nu   B brande-new
     C brand-new   D brand-knew

8. A population   B poplation
     C popalation   D poppulation

9. A defficult   B difficult
     C difficolt   D dificult

10. A ratelsnake   B ratlesnake
     C rattlsnake   D rattlesnake

ANSWERS

1. Ⓐ Ⓑ Ⓒ Ⓓ

2. Ⓐ Ⓑ Ⓒ Ⓓ

3. Ⓐ Ⓑ Ⓒ Ⓓ

4. Ⓐ Ⓑ Ⓒ Ⓓ

5. Ⓐ Ⓑ Ⓒ Ⓓ

6. Ⓐ Ⓑ Ⓒ Ⓓ

7. Ⓐ Ⓑ Ⓒ Ⓓ

8. Ⓐ Ⓑ Ⓒ Ⓓ

9. Ⓐ Ⓑ Ⓒ Ⓓ

10. Ⓐ Ⓑ Ⓒ Ⓓ

Name _____

Unit 6: Writing Activities

WORDS TO WATCH FOR

cheering
stood
interest
hungry
picture
shouted
income
understand
emergency
control

Will This Character Make It into Print?

Create a main character for a story, a person about your age living in the American West. Make the setting the same time period as that in one of your reading selections. Describe your character and setting in detail. Then think of a challenge he or she must face. Plan the beginning, middle, and ending of a story, *but don't write it.* Instead, write your setting and character descriptions on notebook paper, and add the plot outline. Put the paper on a bulletin board along with your classmates' ideas. Finally, choose an idea—your own or that of a classmate—and write the story based on the idea you chose. Use as many of the Words to Watch For as you can.

Tips for Spelling Success

Check a dictionary for the spellings of Western words you're not sure of. Misspelled words distract readers from your story and even discourage them from reading it.

Is This a Great Place or What?

Tips for Spelling Success

- Use a thesaurus to find words for colors and shapes so your description is as clear as you can make it.
- Check for spelling accuracy as you write words you've taken from the thesaurus.

What's the most beautiful, scariest, or most unusual place you've ever dreamed of? Well, here's your chance to describe it in all its glory! First, close your eyes and picture it. Keep it in your mind as long as necessary, so you'll remember every part. Now imagine that you're standing in front of it, and write what's at your feet and on both sides. Raise your head, and describe what's nearby, in the middle of your mental picture. Finally, tell what's in the distance. As you write, describe shapes, textures, colors. Share your special place with a partner or with a small group.

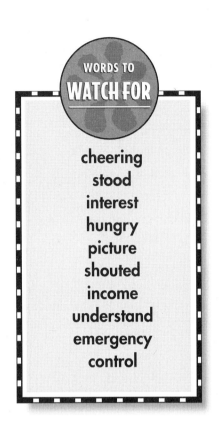

COAST TO COAST Unit 6 Review • Harcourt Brace School Publishers

Name _____

Poems to Travel By

The settlers might have enjoyed hearing some poetry as they traveled west. Work with a group to find poems about places that some might have passed. Ask the school librarian to help you find poetry books to use. Once you've made your choices, draw the route on a large map. Along the route, write the book titles and page numbers of the poems you've chosen. Have one member of your group point out the route for the class. As he or she reaches each place for which you have a poem, group members can take turns reading the poems aloud.

Tips for Spelling Success

As you proofread the poem titles on your map, watch for unusual spellings. Sometimes poets include place names in the titles of their poems, and as you may know, the names of Western settlements were not always spelled in standard English.

What's My Place Name?

Because pioneers had to work hard to survive in the rugged West, most never went to school. But that didn't stop them from naming their towns in very creative ways! Study some maps of the states that were once frontier states. Make a list of towns with unusual names that include a Spelling Word from Unit 6. (Examples: Mexican Hat, Rattlesnake, Island View.) Scramble the letters of each name and challenge a partner to unscramble it and write the name, spelling the Spelling Word correctly. (You might offer hints, such as how many words the name has or which lesson the Spelling Word comes from.)

Tips for Spelling Success

As you list your town names, be sure you copy them correctly. If you scramble the letters in a misspelled word, your partner will not be able to unscramble them to decipher the real town names.

COAST TO COAST Unit 6 Review • Harcourt Brace School Publishers

Spelling Table

THE SPELLING TABLE below lists all the sounds that we use to speak the words of English. Each first column of the table gives the pronunciation symbol for a sound, such as ō. Each second column of the table gives an example of a common word in which this sound appears, such as *open* for the /ō/ sound. Each third column of the table provides examples of the ways that a sound can be spelled, such as *oh, o, oa, ow, oe, ough, ou* and *ew* for the /ō/ sound.

The Sound	As In	Is Spelled As
a	add	cat, laugh, plaid
ā	age	game, rain, day, gauge, steak, weigh, obey, ballet
ä	palm	ah, father, dark, heart
â(r)	care	dare, fair, prayer, where, bear, their
b	bat	big, cabin, rabbit
ch	check	chop, march, catch, nature, mention
d	dog	dig, bad, ladder, called
e	egg	end, met, ready, any, said, says, friend, bury, guess
ē	equal	she, eat, see, people, key, field, machine, receive, piano, city
f	fit	five, offer, cough, half, photo
g	go	gate, bigger, vague, ghost
h	hot	hope, who
i	it	inch, hit, pretty, been, busy, guitar, damage, women, myth
ī	ice	item, fine, pie, high, buy, try, dye, eye, height, island, aisle
j	joy	jump, gem, magic, cage, edge, soldier, graduate, exaggerate
k	keep	king, cat, lock, chorus, account
l	look	let, ball
m	move	make, hammer, calm, climb, condemn
n	nice	new, can, funny, know, gnome, pneumonia

Grade 5 • Harcourt Brace School Publishers

The Sound	As In	Is Spelled As
ng	ri**ng**	thi**ng**, to**ngue**
o	**o**dd	p**o**t, h**o**nor
ō	**o**pen	**oh**, **o**ver, g**o**, **oa**k, gr**ow**, t**oe**, th**ough**, s**ou**l, s**ew**
ô	d**o**g	f**or**, m**ore**, r**oar**, b**a**ll, w**a**lk, d**aw**n, f**au**lt, br**oa**d, **ough**t
oi	**oi**l	n**oi**se, t**oy**
o͝o	t**oo**k	f**oo**t, w**ou**ld, w**o**lf, p**u**ll
o͞o	p**oo**l	c**oo**l, l**o**se, s**ou**p, thr**ough**, r**u**de, d**ue**, fr**ui**t, dr**ew**, can**oe**
ou	**ou**t	**ou**nce, n**ow**, b**ough**
p	**p**ut	**p**in, ca**p**, ha**pp**y
r	**r**un	**r**ed, ca**r**, hu**rr**y, **wr**ist, **rh**yme
s	**s**ee	**s**it, **sc**ene, lo**ss**, li**s**ten, **c**ity, **ps**ychology
sh	ru**sh**	**sh**oe, **su**re, o**ce**an, spe**ci**al, ma**ch**ine, mi**ss**ion, lo**ti**on, pen**si**on, con**sci**ence
t	**t**op	**t**an, kep**t**, bet**t**er, walk**ed**, caugh**t**
th	**th**in	**th**ink, clo**th**
t̶h̶	**th**is	**th**ese, clo**th**ing
u	**u**p	c**u**t, b**u**tter, s**o**me, fl**oo**d, d**oe**s, y**ou**ng
û(r)	b**ur**n	t**ur**n, b**ir**d, w**or**k, **ear**ly, **jour**ney, h**er**d
v	**v**ery	**v**ote, o**v**er, o**f**
w	**w**in	**w**ait, to**w**el
y	**y**et	**y**ear, oni**o**n
yo͞o	**u**se	c**ue**, f**ew**, **you**th, v**iew**, b**eau**tiful
z	**z**oo	**z**ebra, la**z**y, bu**zz**, wa**s**, **s**ci**ss**ors
zh	vi**si**on	plea**s**ure, gara**g**e, televi**si**on
ə		**a**bout, list**e**n, penc**i**l, mel**o**n, circ**u**s

Grade 5 • Harcourt Brace School Publishers

Spelling Dictionary

THIS SECTION OF YOUR BOOK contains your Spelling Dictionary! This is where you'll find all your Spelling Words and WordShopWords.

This is the entry word. It's the word you look up.

Look here to find out how to pronounce the entry word.

These marks indicate the primary and secondary accents.

This abbreviation tells what part of speech the entry word is.

These are two definitions of the entry word.

in·ter·view [in′tər·vyōō′] *n.* a meeting in which one person seeks information from another person: **The reporter asked detailed questions during her** *interview.* —*v.* to ask questions of someone to get information: **Let's** *interview* **the mayor for our school paper.** [21] ◆

These are sample sentences using the entry word.

This is the number of the lesson where you'll find the entry word.

◆ **Interview** comes from the French words meaning "to see" and "one another."

This symbol tells you there is a box below with more information about the entry word.

Use this key to help you figure out the sounds of the letters.

PRONUNCIATION KEY

a	add, map	m	move, seem	u	up, done
ā	ace, rate	n	nice, tin	û(r)	burn, term
â(r)	care, air	ng	ring, song	yōō	fuse, few
ä	palm, father	o	odd, hot	v	vain, eve
b	bat, rub	ō	open, so	w	win, away
ch	check, catch	ô	order, jaw	y	yet, yearn
d	dog, rod	oi	oil, boy	z	zest, muse
e	end, pet	ŏŏ	took, full	zh	vision, pleasure
ē	equal, tree	ōō	pool, food	ə	the schwa,
f	fit, half	ou	pout, now		an unstressed
g	go, log	p	pit, stop		vowel representing
h	hope, hate	r	run, poor		the sound spelled
i	it, give	s	see, pass		**a** in *about*
ī	ice, write	sh	sure, rush		**e** in *sicken*
j	joy, ledge	t	talk, sit		**i** in *possible*
k	cool, take	th	thin, both		**o** in *melon*
l	look, rule	~~th~~	this, bathe		**u** in *circus*

Abbreviations: *n.* noun; *v.* verb; *adj.* adjective; *adv.* adverb; *prep.* preposition; *pron.* pronoun; *interj.* interjection; *conj.* conjunction; *syn.* synonym; *cont.* contraction

A

ac·ro·bat [ak′rə·bat′] *n.* a person who is able to do special movements with the body, such as tumbling, tightrope walking, or swinging from a trapeze: **An** *acrobat* **must be both brave and strong.** [35]

ac·tion [ak′shən] *n.* things that are happening: **Erin joined the** *action* **on the field as Coach Ross sent her into the game.** [19]

ad·di·tion [ə·dish′ən] *n.* the act of adding one thing to another: **We made baked beans in** *addition* **to potato salad.** [19]

ad·mis·sion [ad·mish′ən] *n.* **1.** the price a person must pay to enter a place: **The price of** *admission* **to the concert is ten dollars per person. 2.** the act of admitting something: **The policewoman arrested the robber after his** *admission* **of guilt. 3.** the act of allowing someone to enter a place: **My brother applied for** *admission* **to Harvard.** [19]

ad·ven·ture [ad·ven′chər] *n.* a dangerous, exciting, or very unusual experience: **Our hike to the bottom of the Grand Canyon was quite an** *adventure.* [10]

af·ford [ə·fôrd′] *v.* to have enough money to pay for: **I'd like to buy this bike, but I can** *afford* **only that one.** [25]

Af·ri·ca [af′ri·kə] *n.* the continent south of Europe, between the Atlantic and Indian oceans: **Asia is the only continent larger than** *Africa.* [34]

Af·ri·can [af′ri·kən] *adj.* having to do with the people or culture of Africa: **Tanisha's** *African* **great-grand-father came from Lagos, Nigeria.** [34]

a·grar·i·an [ə·grâr′ē·ən] *adj.* relating to agriculture or farmers: **After Grandpa sold his farm, he missed his** *agrarian* **way of life.** [26]

ag·ri·cul·ture [ag′rə·kul′chər] *n.* the science or business of farming: **Studying** *agriculture* **helps farmers improve their crops.** [25]

air·speed [âr′spēd] *n.* the speed of an aircraft compared to the air through which it moves: **An airplane's** *airspeed* **is faster than its ground speed.** [15]

aisle [īl] *n.* a long, narrow passage to walk down or through: **The flight attendant walked down the** *aisle* **of the plane, serving food.** [33]

al·ley [al′ē] *n.* a narrow street between or behind buildings: **The trash cans are in the** *alley* **behind the restaurant.** [34]

all read·y [ôl′ red′ē] *adj.* completely prepared: **I've got my band uniform, so I'm** *all ready* **for the parade.** [16]

all right [ôl′ rīt′] *adj.* not hurt or sick: **"I'm** *all right,"* **said Ashok. "I just tripped on that tree root."** [16]

all to·geth·er [ôl′ tə·geth′ər] *adv.* as a group: **All** *together,* **there are ten of us in that class.** [16]

a lot [ə lät′] *n.* a large number or amount: **There sure are** *a lot* **of children in first grade this year!** [16]

al·read·y [ôl·red′ē] *adv.* before now or before a certain time: **I've** *already* **done my homework, so I can play until dinner.** [16]

al·though [ôl·thō′] *conj.* in spite of: *Although* **my room isn't large, it's comfortable and warm.** [26]

al·tim·e·ter [al·tim′ət·ər] *n.* an instrument that measures altitude: **An** *altimeter* **measures a plane's distance above the ground.** [15]

al·to·geth·er [ôl′tə·geth′ər] *adv.* completely; entirely: **"This is an** *altogether* **different street," said the lost traveler.** [16]

a·maz·ing [ə·mā′zing] *adj.* wonderful: **A spider web is an** *amazing* **network of silk.** *syns.* remarkable, astonishing [12]

A·mer·i·ca [ə·mer′i·kə] *n.* all the lands of the Western Hemisphere: **Central** *America* **is part of the Western Hemisphere.** [34]

A·mer·i·can [ə·mer′i·kən] *n.* a person born or living in the United States; a person born or living in North or South America: **An** *American* **traveling in Europe should speak several languages.** —*adj.* having to do with the United States: **Not all** *American* **citizens were born in the United States.** [34]

an·cient [ān′shənt] *adj.* having to do with times long ago: **There are many ways to study** *ancient* **civilizations.** [9]

an·gles [ang′gəlz] *n.* areas formed when sets of straight lines or flat surfaces join at given points: **A triangle has three sides and three** *angles.* [2]

an·i·mal [an′ə·məl] *n.* a living being that is not a plant: **As we hiked through the woods, we saw many small** *animals.* —*adj.* **The** *animal* **tracks we saw were made by wolves.** [15]

an·swer [an′sər] *n.* a response to a question or a problem: **Look up the** *answer* **to your question in the encyclopedia.** [33]

an·y·way [en′ē·wā′] *adv.* in any case; anyhow: **I know I've missed the party, but I'll come over** *anyway.* *syn.* nevertheless [16]

an·y way [en′ē wā′] *n.* any possible method: **"Is there** *any way* **to reach your father?" asked Mr. Haddad.** [16]

a	add	ō	open	th	thin
ā	ace	ô	order	th	this
â(r)	care	oi	oil	zh	vision
ä	palm	o͝o	took		
e	end	o͞o	pool	ə	**a** in about
ē	equal	ou	out		**e** in listen
i	it	u	up		**i** in pencil
ī	ice	û(r)	burn		**o** in melon
o	odd	yo͞o	use		**u** in circus

B

a·part·ment [ə·pärt′mənt] *n.* a room or group of rooms to live in: **We live in the *apartment* across the hall from the Matsudas.** [34]

ap·pear [ə·pir′] *v.* to be seen; come into view: **We watched for the school bus to *appear* at the corner.** [25]

ap·pli·ca·tion [ap′li·kā′shən] *n.* a form that must be filled out to do or get something: **Mariana's college *application* has been received.** [32]

ap·ply [ə·plī′] *v.,* **applied, applying.** to make an official request to get or have something, such as a job or a bank loan: **After you *apply* for a job, you may be chosen for an interview.** [32]

A·sia [ā′zhə] *n.* a continent east of Europe and north of the equator: **China, the world's most populous country, is in *Asia*.** [34]

Asia

A·sian [ā′zhən] *adj.* having to do with Asia: **Indonesia is an *Asian* country of more than 13,000 islands.** [34]

ask [ask] *v.* to question to receive information or permission: **Let's *ask* Mom whether we can go to the movies.** *syn.* inquire [1]

ath·lete [ath′lēt] *n.* a person who takes part in sports or games that require skill, speed, and strength: **An *athlete* often does well in many sports.** [32]

ath·let·ic [ath·let′ik] *adj.* having to do with athletes or athletics: **Ryan's *athletic* talent was already apparent when he was five.** [32]

at·ten·tion [ə·ten′shən] *n.* the act of listening, watching, or focusing one's mind on something: **Pay close *attention* to the news so you won't miss anything.** [19]

au·di·ence [ô′dē·əns] *n.* a group of people who watch or listen to a show, game, or other event: **The *audience* applauded when the musicians finished playing.** [20]

a·vail·a·ble [ə·vā′lə·bəl] *adj.* possible to have: **Plenty of towels are *available* in the locker room.** [18]

back·ground [bak′ground′] *n.* the part of a picture or scene behind the main object: **I'll paint Nina's portrait against a *background* of trees.** [31]

back·yard [bak′yärd′] *n.* an area, often with grass, in back of a house or other building: **We barbecue in our *backyard* on warm summer evenings.** [31]

baf·fled [baf′əld] *adj.* confused or puzzled: **When the door didn't open, Rick gave me a *baffled* look.** *syn.* perplexed [14]

bal·ance [bal′əns] *v.* to put or keep in a steady position: ***Balance* this book on your head and walk around the room.** [27]

bar·be·cue [bär′bə·kyoo′] *n.* a meal cooked over hot coals or on an open fire: **At our *barbecue*, Dad cooked chicken and hamburgers on the grill.** (From Spanish *barbacoa*.) [4]

bar·rel [bâr′əl] *v.* to travel very fast: **That's my collie *barreling* through the meadow after a rabbit.** [3]

ba·sin [bā′sən] *n.* a large circular bowl for holding liquids: **Fill the *basin* with water, and take a sponge bath.** [27]

bat·tle [bat′əl] *n.* combat between enemies: **The *battle* ended when the rebels surrendered.** [15]

be·cause [bi·kôz′] *conj.* for the reason that: **Tess is taking her umbrella with her *because* it looks as if it will rain.** [9]

be·come [bi·kum′] *v.,* **became, becoming.** to come to be; to take on a certain state or condition: **Mei-ling is *becoming* quite fluent in English.** [12]

beg·gar [beg′ər] *n.* a person who begs: **The *beggar* asked people for money because he was too sick to work.** [29]

black·smith [blak′smith′] *n.* a person who makes things by heating iron and shaping it with a hammer: **The town *blacksmith* put the first horseshoes on Jeb's colt.** [10]

boil [boil] *v.* to heat a liquid until bubbles form and steam rises: **Add the pasta when the water begins to *boil*. —*n.* a painful red swelling under the skin: **If that's a *boil* on your arm, only a doctor should treat it.** [6]

bold [bōld] *adj.* not afraid; daring and brave: **Because she acted quickly, the *bold* doctor saved her patient's life.** [3]

bought [bôt] *v.* purchased; paid money for: **At the pet store I *bought* fish food and a dog collar.** [7]

brain [brān] *n.* **1.** the mass of nerve tissue inside the skull: **The *brain* controls most of our movements. 2.** *Informal.* a very smart person: **Josh must be a real *brain* to get such good grades!** [2]

brand-new [brand′noo′] *adj.* completely new: ***Brand-new* shoes hurt my feet until I break them in.** [31]

brass [bras] *n.* a yellow metal made of copper and zinc melted together: ***Brass* is strong but easy to work with.—*adj.* made of brass: **Trumpets and tubas are known as *brass* instruments.** [21]

breeze [brēz] *n.* a light, gentle wind: **The trees swayed gently in the soft *breeze*.** (From Spanish *brisa*, "wind.") [4]

brief [brēf] *adj.* short in length or time: **Barry's *brief* letter had only two paragraphs.** [2]

bring [bring] *v.*, **brought, bringing.** to take along or carry: **I'll** *bring* **home some groceries for our dinner.** **brought** [brôt] the past form of **bring: I** *brought* **home the wooden bird I carved at camp.** [7]

brook [brŏŏk] *n.* a small stream of fresh water: **Dad and I fish often in the** *brook* **near our house.** [7]

build [bild] *v.*, **built, building.** to make something by putting parts or materials together: **My sister and I** *build* **sand castles at the beach.** [1]

bunk [bungk] *n.* a narrow bed that is built in or set against a wall like a shelf: **On a ship, a bed is called a** *bunk.* [12]

bur·glar [bûr′glər] *n.* a person who breaks into a building to steal something: **The police caught the** *burglar* **who stole Dad's computer.** [29]

bur·ro [bûr′ō] *n.* a small donkey: **Luis rode the sure-footed** *burro* **to the bottom of the canyon.** [31]

bush [bŏŏsh] *n.* a low plant; a shrub: **No, Dennis, that's a blackberry** *bush,* **not a grapevine.** [7]

bus·y [biz′ē] *adj.* doing something; active: **I'm** *busy* **making cookies, so I can't play now.** [1]

but·ton [but′ən] *n.* a flat, round object that is put onto clothes to fasten parts together: **The** *button* **from Dad's shirt fell off in the washing machine.** [14]

C

cab·in [kab′in] *n.* a small, simple house: **Many settlers lived in log** *cabins* **on the frontier.** [32]

cal·cu·la·tion [kal′kyə·lā′shən] *n.* the act or fact of using arithmetic to obtain the answer to a problem: **By my** *calculation,* **we've gone about five miles.** [2]

ca·noe [kə·nōō′] *n.* a long, narrow boat propelled by one or two paddles: **Connie and I paddled across the lake in a** *canoe.* (From Spanish *canoa.*) [4] ◆

> ◆ **Canoe** is often said to be the first truly American word. When Christopher Columbus landed in the Americas in 1492, he saw the native peoples using a large dugout boat that they called a *canoa.* He and the other sailors had never seen such a boat, and they did not have a word to name it. So they used the word *canoa,* which later became *canoe.*

can·yon [kan′yən] *n.* a deep valley with high, steep sides: **Arizona's Grand** *Canyon* **was formed by the Colorado River.** [14]

ca·pa·ble [kā′pə·bəl] *adj.* able to do something: **Cleon is** *capable* **of doing long division correctly.** [18]

cap·ture [kap′chər] *v.* to catch and hold a person or animal: **Let me know as soon as you** *capture* **that snake!** [10]

car·go [kär′gō] *n.* the goods carried by a ship, plane, or train: **Supplies for the island residents make up most of the ship's** *cargo.* *syn.* freight (From Spanish *cargar,* "to load.") [4]

car·pen·ter [kär′pən·tər] *n.* a person who builds and fixes things made of wood: **Dad hired a** *carpenter* **to make new wood cabinets for our kitchen.** [10]

catch [kach *or* kech] *v.*, **caught, catching. 1.** to take hold of something that is moving: **I'll** *catch* **the next pitch. caught** [kôt] the past form of **catch: Judy** *caught* **the fly ball that ended the baseball game. 2.** to capture or trap: **I** *caught* **a trout in the Holly River. 3.** to reach in time, to board: **Rebecca** *caught* **the bus at the same time every morning. 4.** to become ill or infected with: **Martin** *caught* **the measles from his friend Virgil.** [7]

catch·er [kach′ər *or* kech′ər] *n.* a player on a baseball team whose position is behind home plate: **The** *catcher* **crouched behind home plate and caught the pitch.** [29]

cat·tle [kat′əl] *n.* cows and steers raised for meat, milk, and hides: **Among the grazing** *cattle* **were several new calves.** [15]

cel·e·bra·tion [sel′ə·brā′shən] *n.* the honoring of a certain day or occasion with special activities: **We're having a big party in** *celebration* **of Grandpa's sixty-fifth birthday.** [19]

cen·tu·ry [sen′chə·rē] *n.* a period of one hundred years: **The twentieth** *century* **began in the year 1901.** [35]

chain [chān] *n.* a row of rings or links joined to one another: **Anaba wore a silver** *chain* **around her neck.** —*v.* to fasten or hold with a chain: **If you** *chain* **your car to our truck, we'll tow it to the garage.** [2]

change [chānj] *v.*, **changed, changing. 1.** to make or become different: **Frank's frown** *changed* **to a smile when he saw the sun come out. Shani** *changed* **her mind and ordered a salad instead of fries. 2.** to put on other clothes or coverings: **I** *changed* **into my softball uniform at home. 3.** to exchange money, such as one country's currency for another's: **The bank** *changed* **my dollars into Swiss francs.** —*adj.* having become different: **Mr. Hazra is a** *changed* **man since his recovery from the accident.** [12]

a	add	ō	open	th	thin
ā	ace	ô	order	th	this
â(r)	care	oi	oil	zh	vision
ä	palm	ŏŏ	took		
e	end	ōō	pool	ə	**a** in about
ē	equal	ou	out		**e** in listen
i	it	u	up		**i** in pencil
ī	ice	û(r)	burn		**o** in melon
o	odd	yōō	use		**u** in circus

chap·ter [chap′tər] *n.* one section of a book: **I looked at the last** *chapter* **of the book to see how the story ended.** [14]

chat·ter [chat′ər] *v.* to talk much or rapidly about unimportant matters: **Tamiko and I** *chatter* **about small things, but we have serious talks, too.** [4]

chat·ter·ing [chat′ər·ing] *adj.* making quick, rattling sounds: **Sheila stood in the snow, her teeth** *chattering* **from the cold.** —*n.* quick, rattling sounds: **The** *chattering* **must be coming from those chipmunks.** [23]

cheeks [chēks] *n.* the wide, fleshy parts of the face between the nose and the ears: **The baby had blond hair, blue eyes, and rosy** *cheeks.* [2]

cheese [chēz] *n.* a food made from curdled milk: **Dad doesn't eat** *cheese* **because it upsets his stomach.** —*adj.* made with cheese: *Cheese* **pizza is my favorite Friday night dinner.** [2]

chi·li [chil′ē] *n.* a spicy dish flavored with red pepper, usually made with meat and beans: **Lupe use hot peppers and black beans to make** *chili.* From Spanish *chile.*) [4]

choc·o·late [chok′lət *or* chôk′lət] *n.* a food product made of ground cacao beans, used in candies and in baking: **Did you know that** *chocolate* **comes from beans?** —*adj.* flavored with or made from chocolate: **My brother Carlos enjoys** *chocolate* **ice cream with pecans.** (From Spanish *chocolate.*) [4]

cho·sen [chō′zən] *adj.* picked or selected from a group: **The** *chosen* **player ran to join her team.** [27]

cir·cle [sûr′kəl] *n.* a group of people who share the same interests: **We always welcome newcomers into our** *circle* **of friends.** [8]

cir·cus [sûr′kəs] *n.* a show with clowns, acrobats, trained animals, and other performers: **The clowns are my favorite performers at the** *circus.* —*adj.* **Would you like to see my new** *circus* **act?** [25]

civ·il [siv′əl] *adj.* having to do with a citizen or citizenship: *Civil* **laws involve the private rights of citizens.** [15]

cloth [klôth] *n.* material made by weaving or knitting fibers: **Dad made me a Halloween costume out of cotton** *cloth.* [7]

clothes [klōz] *n.* things worn to cover the body: **You'll need heavy winter** *clothes* **to play in the snow.** [9]

clouds [kloudz] *n.* masses of water droplets in the form of mist or haze floating high in the sky: *Clouds* **that look like a flock of sheep are a sign of rain.** [6]

clue [kloō] *n.* something that helps solve a problem or mystery: **A fingerprint was the** *clue* **that helped the detective solve her case.** [3]

co·ci·na [kō·sē′nə] *n.* a Spanish word meaning *kitchen:* **Julia helped Mrs. Rodriguez make dinner in the** *cocina.* [31]

col·umn [kol′əm] *n.* **1.** a tall, slender post or pillar that supports a roof or other part of a building: **Each**

column bears part of the building's weight. **2.** a narrow vertical section of words or figures: **Add the figures in the first** *column.* **3.** a regular article or feature in a newspaper or magazine: **The reporter writes a daily** *column* **for the newspaper.** [33]

comb [kōm] *v.* to arrange or style the hair, using a strip of hard material that has teeth: **I always** *comb* **my hair after I wash my face.** [3]

com·fort·a·ble [kum′fər·tə·bəl *or* kumf′tər·bəl] *adj.* giving comfort: **This is the most** *comfortable* **chair I've ever sat in!** [18]

com·mon [kom′ən] *adj.* shared by two or more people or groups: **Sewing is our** *common* **interest, so we often work together.** [25]

com·pete [kəm·pēt′] *n.* to take part in a contest or game, attempting to do better than all the others: **We'll all** *compete* **in the charity fun run.** [32]

com·pet·i·tive [kəm·pet′ə·tiv] *adj.* **1.** having to do with or using competition: **Many college admissions are decided by** *competitive* **exams. 2.** liking to win or compete: **Ed is such a** *competitive* **player that he never gives up during a game.** [32]

com·plex [kəm·pleks′] *adj.* hard to explain or understand; complicated: **Compared to a typewriter, a computer is a very** *complex* **machine.** [26]

com·po·si·tion [kom′pə·zish′ən] *n.* something that is put together: **Each musician will play one** *composition* **during the recital.** [20]

con·duc·tor [kən·duk′tər] *n.* a person in charge of passengers on a train, bus, or streetcar: **The train** *conductor* **called "All aboard!"** [33]

con·fu·sion [kən·fyoō′zhən] *n.* an uncertain or disordered situation: **Tad somehow got lost in the** *confusion* **on the field.** [19]

Con·gress [kong′gris] *n.* the lawmaking branch of the United States government: **The United States** *Congress* **promised to pass laws to balance the nation's budget.** [26]

con·sid·er·a·ble [kən·sid′ər·ə·bəl] *adj.* worth noticing or considering; rather large: **The blizzard left a** *considerable* **amount of snow in West Haven.** [18]

con·sole [kon′sōl] *n.* a cabinet that holds electronic devices: **The engineer turned a dial on the** *console* **to soften the studio noise.** [18]

con·trap·tion [kən·trap′shən] *n.* a gadget or device: **A towel on a long pole was the maid's** *contraption* **for dusting high corners.** [23]

con·trol [kən·trōl′] *v.,* **controlled, controlling.** to direct the course of; regulate: **I** *control* **my urge to snack by going for a walk. controlled** [kən·trōld′] —*adj.* done according to standards or regulations: **That was a** *controlled* **experiment.** [13]

coun·cil [koun′səl] *n.* a group of people who meet to decide certain things: **The city** *council* **passed a recycling bill.** [15]

cou·ple [kup′əl] *n.* two people or things thought of as forming a pair; two people or things together: **Mr. and Mrs. Cheng are a married** *couple.* [15]

cour·te·ous [kûr′tē·əs] *adj.* considerate toward other people: **The** *courteous* **man stood and gave Grandma his seat on the bus.** *syn.* polite [6]

cov·er [kuv′ər] *v.,* covered, covering. **1.** to spread over the surface of: *Cover* **the icy steps with sand. 2.** to place or put something over or on: **Pat** *covered* **the baby with a blanket.** [13]

coy·o·te [kī·ō′tē *or* kī′ōt] *n.* a wolflike animal found in central and western North America: **The** *coyote* **sat and howled under the desert moon.** (From Spanish *coyote.*) [4]

crack·le [krak′əl] *v.,* crackled, crackling. to make a quick, sharp, snapping sound: **My breakfast cereal began** *crackling* **as soon as I poured milk on it.** [23]

creak [krēk] *v.,* creaked, creaking. to make a sharp, squeaking sound: **The old stairs were** *creaking* **as Claire climbed up to the attic.** [23]

cre·ate [krē·āt′] *v.* to cause something new to come into being: **The artist will** *create* **a statue of a tiger for the entrance to the zoo.** [28]

cre·a·tion [krē·ā′shən] *n.* something new that has been brought into being: **Arnie's pyramid made of craft sticks was an original** *creation.* [23]

crea·ture [krē′chər] *n.* any living person or animal: **This elephant is the largest** *creature* **I've ever seen!** [10]

cried [krīd] *v.* the past form of **cry:** to call loudly: **Masako** *cried,* **"Has anyone seen my winter coat?"** [12]

cross [krôs] *v.* to go from one side of something to the other: **We'll** *cross* **the Atlantic Ocean when we fly from New York to Paris.** [7]

cru·el [krōō′əl] *adj.* willing to give pain and suffering to others; very unkind: **It's** *cruel* **to tell Ralph that the cookies he baked are as hard as rocks.** [28]

cul·ture [kul′chər] *n.* all the beliefs, habits, and customs that make a certain group of people distinct from other groups: **The Hopi nation has had an advanced** *culture* **for centuries.** [10]

dance [dans] *v.* to move the body in time to music: **We will** *dance* **as soon as the music starts.** —*n.* a party where people dance: **The** *dance* **will take place on Friday night.** [1]

dash·board [dash′bôrd′] *n.* a panel in an automobile directly in front of the driver: **Check the speedometer on the** *dashboard* **to see how fast we're going.** [15]

daugh·ter [dô′tər] *n.* a female child: **My cousin Marlene is my Aunt Sue's** *daughter.* [14]

de·cide [di·sīd′] *v.,* decided, deciding. to make up one's mind: **When he saw the weeds, Dad** *decided* **to do some yard work.** [22]

deck [dek] *n.* one of the levels on a ship: **Passengers waved from the main** *deck* **as the ship left port.** [12]

de·clare [di·klâr′] *v.* to claim; to say: **My parents** *declare* **that I know more about computers than they do.** [8]

de·duct [di·dukt′] *v.* to take away one amount from another: **The store will** *deduct* **20 percent from every sale item.** *syn.* subtract [22]

de·fense [di·fens′] *n.* something that defends, guards, or protects: **Janell came to our** *defense* **because she knew we weren't guilty.** —*adj.* having to do with the armed services: **My mom has a** *defense* **job at our local air force base.** [22]

de·gree [di·grē′] *n.* **1.** one number or unit of a system used for measuring things: **A body temperature of 99.6°F is one** *degree* **above normal for most people. 2.** an official title given for completing a certain course of study: **My sister Tala will receive her engineering** *degree* **in May.** [22]

de·light [di·līt′] *n.* great pleasure or happiness; joy: **Donna takes** *delight* **in gardening because she loves plants.** [22]

del·ta [del′tə] *n.* a mass of sand, mud, and earth at the mouth of a river, forming a triangle: **Muddy banks marked the** *delta* **where the river flowed into the ocean.** [28]

de·mand [di·mand′] *v.* to ask for something in a strong, forceful way: **The losing candidate may** *demand* **a recount of the votes.** [22]

den·tist [den′tist] *n.* a person who is professionally trained to take care of people's teeth: **My** *dentist* **congratulated me for having no cavities.** [29]

de·scribe [di·scrīb′] *v.* to give a picture of a thing in words; write or tell about: *Describe* **your lost dog so I'll know what he looks like.** [22]

des·ert [dez′ərt] *n.* a very dry area of land with few or no plants growing: **A cactus can live in a** *desert* **because it doesn't need much water.** —*adj.* having few or no plants: **What would you do if you were stranded on a** *desert* **island?** [27]

a	add	ō	open	th	thin
ā	ace	ô	order	th	this
â(r)	care	oi	oil	zh	vision
ä	palm	o͝o	took		
e	end	o͞o	pool	ə	**a** in about
ē	equal	ou	out		**e** in listen
i	it	u	up		**i** in pencil
ī	ice	û(r)	burn		**o** in melon
o	odd	yo͞o	use		**u** in circus

de·sign [di·zīn′] *n.* a certain pattern of lines, colors, or shapes: **The flowers on the plate are part of its** *design.* [22]

de·tails [di·tālz′ *or* dē′tālz] *n.* small or less important points or facts: **The story outline didn't include many** *details.* [22]

de·ter·mined [di·tûr′mind] *adj.* having decided or settled definitely: **Araceli was** *determined* **to travel by plane.** [14]

de·vel·op [di·vel′əp] *v.* **1.** to come to be or have: **A plumbing problem will** *develop* **if this sink remains clogged. 2.** to use chemicals on film to make pictures appear: **Please** *develop* **this film as soon as possible.** [22]

de·vout [di·vout′] *adj.* very religious; sincere in belief: *Devout* **people are of many religious faiths.** [26]

di·a·logue [dī′ə·lôg′ *or* dī′ə·log′] *n.* the words spoken by characters in a story or play: **Every time Gene sees a play, he talks theater** *dialogue* **for a week.** [4]

di·a·ry [dī′rē *or* dī′ə·rē] *n.* a daily written record of a person's thoughts, feelings, and experiences: **Writing in my** *diary* **is like talking to a friend.** [4]

di·et [dī′ət] *n.* the food and drink consumed by a person or animal: **A healthful** *diet* **includes plenty of fruits and vegetables.** [28]

dif·fi·cult [dif′ə·kult] *adj.* hard to do or understand: **Italian is not a** *difficult* **language to learn.** [35]

di·no·saur [dī′nə·sôr′] *n.* one of a group of creatures that lived on earth millions of years ago, but have completely died out: **A tyrannosaur was a huge** *dinosaur* **that walked on two legs.** [35]

dinosaur

di·rec·tion [di·rek′shən] *n.* **1.** the act or fact of directing; being under someone's control: **We practiced the play under the** *direction* **of our teacher. 2.** the way in which something moves or faces: **In which** *direction* **should we go now?** [19]

di·rec·tor [di·rek′tər] *n.* a person in charge of a play, movie, or television show: **The** *director* **called "Cut!" when the star forgot his lines.** [29]

dirt [dûrt] *n.* soil; earth: **My dog got his paws muddy by digging in some** *dirt.* [8]

dis·a·bil·i·ty [dis′ə·bil′ə·tē] *n.* a condition that prevents a person from doing something: **Deafness isn't a** *disability* **for Jeff since he learned sign language.** [22]

dis·ad·van·tage [dis′əd·van′tij] *n.* a condition that makes something less attractive or appealing: **Noise is a** *disadvantage* **of living near the airport.** [22]

dis·ap·point·ed [dis′ə·point′id] *v.* having failed to get what one wanted or hoped for: **We were all** *disappointed* **when our trip was canceled.** [22]

dis·con·nect [dis′kə·nekt′] *v.* to break a connection: **If we** *disconnect* **these wires, the lights won't go on.** [1]

dis·count [dis′kount] *n.* an amount subtracted from the regular price of something: **I got a** *discount* **on my bike because the store was having a sale.** [22]

dis·play [dis·plā′] *v.* to show for others to see; put in view: **Aunt Emma will** *display* **her baked goods at the county fair.** —*n.* the act of showing something: **Is it dark enough yet for the fireworks** *display* **to begin?** [26]

dis·sat·is·fied [dis·sat′is·fīd′] *adj.* not happy about something: **Dad was** *dissatisfied* **with the way I painted the bookcase.** [22]

dis·turb [dis·tûrb′] *v.,* disturbed, disturbing. to break in on; interrupt; bother: **Dad is not to be** *disturbed* **while he's napping.** [22]

di·vide [di·vīd′] *v.* to show how many of one number is contained in another number: *Divide* **the cost by the number of ounces to get the cost per ounce.** [32]

di·vi·sion [di·vizh′ən] *n.* in arithmetic, the process of dividing one number into another: **Don solved the problem by using long** *division.* [2, 32]

does [duz] *v.* a form of the word **do** used with *she, he, it,* or the name of a person: **How** *does* **the magician make the rabbit disappear?** [1]

door·way [dôr′wā′] *n.* an opening that is closed by a door: **I stood in the** *doorway* **waving good-bye as Anna drove away.** [31]

dou·ble [dub′əl] *adj.* two times as many or two times as much: **This is a** *double*-**sided ax.** [15]

doz·en [duz′ən] *n.* a group or set of twelve things: **Most eggs are packaged by the** *dozen.* [14]

drag·on [drag′ən] *n.* an imaginary animal that breathes out smoke and fire: **The hero in the legend killed a** *dragon* **to save a beautiful maiden.** [14]

dream [drēm] *n.* pictures and thoughts that come to the mind during sleep: **A nightmare is just a bad** *dream.* —*v.* to have a dream or daydream: **I knew I would** *dream* **about candy just before Halloween!** [2]

driv·er [drī′vər] *n.* a person who operates a car or other vehicle: **Our bus** *driver* **obeys the traffic laws.** [29]

drown [droun] *v.* to die because water fills the lungs so that one cannot breathe: **Ruth dived into the pool and saved a child who had begun to** *drown.* [6]

ear·nest [ûr′nist] *adj.* strong in purpose; serious and sincere: **Tranh made an** *earnest* **apology when he broke his father's compact disc player.** [14]

earn·ings [ûr´ningz] *n.* the money that is made from working or doing business: **I deposit the *earnings* I get from my paper route into a savings account.** [8]

earth·quake [ûrth´kwāk´] *n.* the shaking or trembling of the earth: **The *earthquake* shook the freeway overpass until it crumbled.** [31]

ed·i·tor [ed´i·tər] *n.* a person who improves and corrects written material to prepare it for publication: **The first thing the *editor* did was correct my grammar.** [9]

ed·u·ca·tion [ej´o̅o̅·kā´shən] *n.* the process of learning; the development of knowledge and skills: **Learning about other cultures is part of a student's *education*.** [19]

ef·fort [ef´ərt] *n.* the use of work or energy to do something: **Lian believes that learning is worth the *effort* of studying.** [25]

em·bark [im·bärk´] *v.* to set out on a journey: **Pack plenty of supplies before you *embark*.** [7]

em·ploy·ee [im·ploi´ē] *n.* a person who is paid to work for someone else: **Mr. Burns is an *employee* at my parents' grocery store.** [6]

em·ploy·er [im·ploi´ər] *n.* a person or company paying others to work: **My brother's *employer* is Mrs. Carbone, who owns the bakery.** [6]

en·er·gy [en´ər·jē] *n.* the power to cause things to move or do other kinds of work: **We can save *energy* by setting the thermostat below 68 degrees in winter.** [35]

en·gi·neer [en´jə·nir´] *n.* a person who is trained to design and build roads, bridges, and electrical equipment: **An *engineer* designed this bridge to cross the bay.** [29]

Eng·land [ing´glənd] *n.* the largest division of the United Kingdom, in the southern part of the island of Great Britain: **The English Channel separates *England* from France.** [34]

Eng·lish [ing´glish] *adj.* having to do with the people or culture of England: **Charles Dickens was an *English* author.** —*n.* the language which is spoken in England as well as in other countries once under British rule: **English is a wonderful but sometimes confusing language.** [34]

en·ter [en´tər] *v.* to come or go into: **The teams *entered* the stadium as their names were announced.** [13]

e·va·sive·ly [i·vā´siv·lē] *adv.* not frankly or directly: **When asked about the stolen car, the man answered *evasively*.** [13]

e·ven [ē´vən] *adv.* at the same time; while: **Stacy reads all the time, *even* during dinner.** [27]

eve·ry·bod·y [ev´rē·bud´ē *or* ev´rē·bod´ē] *pron.* every person: **There are no absences, so *everybody* in our class is present today.** [31]

eve·ry·day [ev´rē·dā´] *adj.* ordinary: **These are my *everyday* clothes; I save my good clothes for special occasions.** [16]

eve·ry day [ev´rē dā´] *adv.* each and all days: **I make my bed *every day* before breakfast.** [16]

eve·ry·one [ev´rē·wun´] *pron.* every person: ***Everyone* wishes that summer vacation were here.** [16]

eve·ry one [ev´rē wun´] *n.* all the items in a group: **After we had picked the berries, we saw that Ken had eaten *every one*.** [16]

e·vil [ē´vəl] *adj.* very bad: **The hero of the story conquered the *evil* king who had tried to kill him.** *syn.* wicked [15]

ex·am·ple [ig·zam´pəl] *n.* one of a group of things, used to show what the others are like: **A daffodil is an *example* of a spring-blooming flower.** [35]

ex·cit·ed [ik·sī´tid] *adj.* having or showing strong and lively feelings: **The night before my birthday party, I was too *excited* to sleep.** [9]

ex·plode [ik·splōd´] *v.* to break apart suddenly and violently: **I like to watch fireworks *explode* on the Fourth of July.** [26]

ex·tra [ek´strə] *adj.* more than is usual or needed; additional: **Give Raja *extra* food because he's very hungry.** [26]

fact [fakt] *n.* something that is known to be true or real; something that exists or that has happened: **It is a *fact* that the sun is a star.** [1]

fac·tor [fak´tər] *v.* to include some amount in a calculation: **The price is reasonable when you *factor* in the discount.** [14]

false [fôls] *adj.* not true or real: **The robber made a *false* statement to the police.** [7]

farm·land [färm´land´] *n.* land used for growing crops: **Good *farmland* will produce rich crops if it's well cared for.** [31]

far·ther [fär´thər] *adv.* more distant; more far: **Buy a house *farther* out in the country if you want to have horses.** [26]

a	add	ō	open	th	thin
ā	ace	ô	order	th	this
â(r)	care	oi	oil	zh	vision
ä	palm	o̅o̅	took		
e	end	o̅o̅	pool	ə	**a** in about
ē	equal	ou	out		**e** in listen
i	it	u	up		**i** in pencil
ī	ice	û(r)	burn		**o** in melon
o	odd	yo̅o̅	use		**u** in circus

fas·ten [fas′ən] *v.* to close up, attach, or connect; make fast: **Dad** *fastened* **the shutters on the windows with strong hinges.** [1]

fa·vor·a·ble [fāv′rə·bəl] *adj.* in one's favor; promising; encouraging: **Today's weather isn't** *favorable* **for a picnic.** [18]

fav·o·rite [fāv′rit] *adj.* best-liked; favored over others: **I like to paint trees because green is my** *favorite* **color.** [35]

fea·ture [fē′chər] *n.* **1.** a single part of the face or body: **Mom says my dark-brown eyes are my best** *feature.* **2.** a quality or part that stands out: **A blizzard is a standard** *feature* **of northern winters. 3.** a full-length movie: **The theater showed two previews before the main** *feature.* —*adj.* a special story in a newspaper or magazine: **Andrea is writing a** *feature* **story for our local newspaper.** —*v.* to give importance to: **The magazine will** *feature* **photos of the marathon.** [10]

fel·low [fel′ō] *n.* any man or boy: **That** *fellow* **looks just like my brother Paolo.** [25]

fierce [firs] *adj.* very strong or dangerous: **No one would guess that such** *fierce* **barking could come from a tiny poodle.** [6]

fi·es·ta [fē·es′tə] *n.* a day or time to celebrate something: **We'll serve tacos and tamales at the** *fiesta.* (Spanish for *feast, festival.*) [31]

fin·ish [fin′ish] *v.* to dispose of entirely; use up: **I'll** *finish* **your dessert if you don't want it.** *syn.* terminate —*n.* the final coat or surface of a thing: **What kind of** *finish* **will you put on the table?** [27]

fire·place [fīr′plās′] *n.* an open place at the bottom of a chimney to make a fire: **The maple logs crackled in the brick** *fireplace.* [31]

flag·ship [flag′ship′] *n.* the ship that carries the commander of a fleet and flies his flag: **The** *flagship* **was well armed to protect the commander on board.** [19] ◆

> ◆ **Flagship** comes from the fact that in earlier times the commander of a fleet of warships had a special flag. This flag flew on the ship on which the commander sailed. This was usually the biggest and most important ship in the whole fleet. From this we get the idea that a *flagship* is the largest, best, or most important one in a group: **That company owns many clothing stores, but its** *flagship* **store is in a six-story building on Fifth Avenue in New York City.**

flash·light [flash′līt′] *n.* a small battery-powered electric light that is usually held in the hand: **I shone my** *flashlight* **on the rustling grasses and saw a rabbit hop away.** [31]

fla·vor [flā′vər] *n.* **1.** the way in which a food is sensed by the mouth; a particular taste: **The ice cream** *flavor* **of the month is black cherry. 2.** a special quality that makes a thing different from others: **The city of Santa Fe has a southwestern** *flavor.* [14]

fleet [flēt] *n.* a group of warships under one command: **A** *fleet* **of tall ships sailed into the harbor.** [19]

flus·tered [flus′tərd] *adj.* not calm; nervous or confused: **Marcelo became** *flustered* **when he couldn't find his plane ticket.** [13]

flute [floot] *n.* a musical instrument that is shaped like a tube and is played by blowing across a hole in one end while covering other holes with the fingers: **Breath control and finger movement are important in playing the** *flute.* [3]

folks [fōks] *n.* people in general: **The** *folks* **who live next door are our neighbors.** [3]

for·get [fər·get′] *v.,* **forgot, forgetting.** to be unable to call to mind something that was once known; not remember: **Tandra kept** *forgetting* **her new phone number until she found a way to remember it.** [13]

for·mal [fôr′məl] *adj.* following customs or rules: **Rita learned to play the guitar without** *formal* **instruction.** [15]

for·tress [fôr′tris] *n.* a stronghold; a fort, especially a large fort: **The king built a** *fortress* **to protect the city from invaders.** [27]

for·ty [fôr′te] *adj.* the number that is equal to four times ten; 40: **Dad will be** *forty* **years old in the year 2000.** [8]

for·ward [fôr′wərd] *adv.* at or toward the front: **Face** *forward,* **and don't look behind you.** [25]

freeze [frēz] *v.,* **froze, frozen, freezing.** to become covered or filled with ice: **This mammoth was** *frozen* **in a glacier millions of years ago.** [14]

front [frunt] *n.* the part that faces forward or comes at the beginning; the opposite side from the back: **Emilio has his tickets because he was at the** *front* **of the line when the box office opened.** —*adj.* on or near this place: **I like to sit in the** *front* **seat of the car beside Dad.** [1]

fron·tier [frun·tir′] *n.* a region on the edge of some unsettled land: **The pioneers who settled the western** *frontier* **had a very hard life.** [32]

frown [froun] *n.* a wrinkling of the forehead in thought or displeasure: **I always** *frown* **when I think about washing the dishes.** [6]

fro·zen [frō′zən] *v.* the past form of **freeze:** to become chilled or solid with cold: **The lake was** *frozen,* **and the whole town came out to skate.** [14]

fruit [froot] *n.* a sweet, juicy part of a plant that is good to eat: **Gina likes all kinds of** *fruit,* **but green grapes are her favorite.** [3]

fu·el [fyōō′əl] *n.* a substance that is burned to provide heat or power: **Please buy unleaded *fuel* for the new car.** [28]

full [fŏol] *adj.* holding as much or as many as possible: **The fishing boat made a good catch and returned with a *full* load.** [7]

fur·ni·ture [fûr′ni·chər] *n.* movable items, such as tables, chairs, and beds, that make a place comfortable: **Our dogs aren't allowed on the living room *furniture*.** [10]

fu·se·lage [fyōō′sə·läzh′] *n.* the main body of an airplane that holds the crew, passengers, and cargo: **Our seats were in the *fuselage* of the huge jet airliner.** [15]

G

gath·er [gath′ər] *v.* to bring or come together: **We're *gathering* in the gym for a special assembly program.** [13]

ge·om·e·try [jē·äm′ə·trē] *n.* the branch of mathematics that deals with the study of points, lines, angles, and shapes: **At the age of nine, Julie was already learning *geometry*.** [2]

ges·ture [jes′chər] *n.* a movement of the hand, head, or body to show how a person feels or thinks: **Waving one's hand is a *gesture* that can mean hello or goodbye.** [10]

gi·ant [jī′ənt] *adj.* very, very large: **Some *giant* redwood trees are 300 feet tall.** [28]

gnaw [nô] *v.* to chew so as to wear away: **My dog can *gnaw* on a bone for hours.** [33]

gnome [nōm] *n.* in fables and fairy tales, a dwarf or other tiny creature who lives under the ground and guards treasures: **The *gnome* cried when his treasure chest disappeared.** [33]

goal·ie [gō′lē] *n.* an informal word for *goalkeeper,* the player who defends the team's goal in sports such as soccer and hockey: **A hockey *goalie* wears thick padding for protection from sticks and pucks.** [29]

gone [gän] *adj.* no longer present: **The trash is *gone* now, because the garbage truck just took it away.** [1]

grass·lands [gras′landz′] *n.* land with grass growing on it; prairie: **The lioness prowled the *grasslands* looking for prey.** [28]

Greece [grēs] *n.* a country in southeastern Europe that includes the southern end of the Balkan Peninsula and several islands in the Aegean Sea: **Ancient *Greece* was divided into independent city-states.** [34]

Greek [grēk] *adj.* having to do with the people or culture of Greece: **Plato and Aristotle were ancient *Greek* philosophers.** [34]

grind [grīnd] *v.* to crush or chop into small pieces or fine powder: **We *grind* our pepper from whole peppercorns.** [23]

grum·ble [grum′bəl] *v.,* grumbled, grumbling. showing unhappiness or discontent; complaining in a low, angry voice: **Bob sat at the table *grumbling* until I made him some lunch.** [6]

gur·gle [gûr′gəl] *v.* to make a low, uneven, bubbling sound: **My cat Cinnamon likes to hear water *gurgle* down the drain.** [23]

H

ha·ci·en·da [hä′sē·en′də] *n.* a ranch house in Mexico, South America, or the southwestern United States: **Conchita lives at her family's hacienda in Argentina.** (From an old Spanish word meaning "things to be done.") [31]

half [haf] *n.* one of two equal parts of something: **Since you forgot your lunch, I'll give you *half* of my sandwich.** [33]

hap·pen [hap′ən] *v.* to take place; come about: **Tell me what *happened* during your camping trip.** [13]

health [helth] *n.* the condition in which the body and mind are free from sickness and injury: **Eating well and exercising are important for good *health*.** [1]

honk [hongk] *v.* to make or cause to make a loud, harsh sound: **Mrs. Wang *honked* the car horn when a truck swerved into our lane.** [23]

hood [hŏod] *n.* a protective covering for the head and neck: **Wear a sweatshirt with a *hood* to keep your head warm.** [7]

hor·ri·ble [hôr′ə·bəl] *adj.* **1.** causing horror; frightening or shocking: **The pilot pulled the plane up just in time to avoid a *horrible* crash. 2.** *Informal.* very bad or unpleasant: **That *horrible* photo is on Dad's driver's license.** [18]

hos·pi·tal [hos′pit·əl] *n.* a place where doctors, nurses, and other medical workers provide care and treatment for the sick and injured: **Pete went to the *hospital* to have his tonsils removed.** [35]

a	add	ō	open	th	thin
ā	ace	ô	order	th	this
â(r)	care	oi	oil	zh	vision
ä	palm	ŏo	took		
e	end	ōo	pool	ə	**a** in about
ē	equal	ou	out		**e** in listen
i	it	u	up		**i** in pencil
ī	ice	û(r)	burn		**o** in melon
o	odd	yōo	use		**u** in circus

how·ev·er [hou·ev′ər] *conj.* even so; in any case: **I like my job;** *however,* **I wish my salary were higher.** *syn.* nevertheless [35]

hu·man [hyo͞o′mən] *adj.* having to do with a person or people: **A person is a** *human* **being.** [14]

hymn [him] *n.* a song of praise to God: **The church service ended with the singing of a** *hymn.* [33]

I

il·lus·tra·tor [i′ləs·trā′tər] *n.* a person who adds pictures to books or other written work in order to explain, decorate, or make them more interesting: **Mr. Swanson is a famous** *illustrator* **of children's books.** [9]

im·prove [im·pro͞ov′] *v.* to become or make better: **Fertilizing an orange tree will** *improve* **the quality of its fruit.** [26]

in·clude [in·klo͞od′] *v.* to have as a part; have within it: **The summer months** *include* **August.** [21]

in·crease [in·krēs′ *or* in′krēs] *v.* to make or become larger in size or amount: **We'll** *increase* **the size of our house by adding another bedroom.** [26]

in·for·ma·tion [in′fər·mā′shən] *n.* a group of facts known about something: **Kim needs to collect more** *information* **about snakes for her science report.** [19]

in·stead [in·sted′] *adv.* in place of something else: **Kay buys pretzels** *instead* **of candy because she prefers lowfat snacks.** [26]

in·struc·tions [in·struk′shənz] *n.* the steps involved in learning to do something; directions: **Read the** *instructions* **before you try to program the VCR.** [19]

in·su·lat·ed [in′sə·lāt′əd] *adj.* being covered, filled, or surrounded with a special material that slows or stops the flow of heat, electricity, or sound: *Insulated* **wires help prevent fires and electrical shocks.** [1]

in·ter·me·di·ate [in′tər·mē′dē·it] *adj.* in the middle; between the first and the last stages: **To take** *intermediate* **Spanish, you must first complete beginning Spanish.** [21]

in·ter·rupt [in′tə·rupt′] *v.* to stop or break in on something: **An afternoon fire drill will** *interrupt* **our math lesson.** [21]

in·ter·view [in′tər·vyo͞o′] *n.* a meeting in which one person seeks information from another person: **The reporter asked detailed questions during her** *interview.* —*v.* to ask questions of someone to get information: **Let's** *interview* **the mayor for our school paper.** [21] ◆

> ◆ **Interview** comes from the French words meaning "to see" and "one another."

in·vent [in·vent′] *v.,* **invented, inventing.** to make or think of for the first time; create something new: **In his New Haven shop Eli Whitney** *invented* **a machine to process cotton.** [21]

in·ven·tion [in·ven′chən] *n.* something brought into being for the first time: **The telephone, Alexander Graham Bell's** *invention,* **greatly influences our lives.** [23]

in·vite [in·vīt′] *v.,* **invited, inviting.** to ask someone to come somewhere or do something: **All our relatives were** *invited* **to graduation.** [21]

is·land [ī′lənd] *n.* a body of land completely surrounded by water: **The** *island* **of Bermuda is only 22 miles long.** —*adj.* a place with the qualities of an island: **Cuba is an** *island* **country in the Caribbean Sea.** [33]

island

i·tem [ī′təm] *n.* a single thing: **Bread is the only** *item* **I need from the grocery store.** [27]

J

Ja·pan [jə·pan′] *n.* a country east of the mainland of Asia, made up of four large islands and several smaller ones: **Honshu is the largest of the islands that make up** *Japan.* [34]

Jap·a·nese [jap′ə·nēz′] *adj.* having to do with the people or culture of Japan: **Rice is important to the** *Japanese* **diet.** [34]

jour·nal [jûr′nəl] *n.* a record of daily events that someone writes about his or her life or work: **Jesse writes in his** *journal* **every day.** [4]

juice [jo͞os] *n.* the liquid extracted from fruits, vegetables, or meats: **Guadalupe had a glass of orange** *juice* **with her breakfast.** [3]

K

knight [nīt] *n.* a soldier in the Middle Ages who fought on horseback: **Only a** *knight* **could wear a suit of armor.** [2]

L

land·scape [land′skāp′] *n.* a view of a certain area of land, or a picture of such a view: **Mountains, valleys, and rivers beautify the *landscape*.** [29]

las·so [las′ō] *n.* a long rope with a loop at one end that can be tightened: **The rider twirled his *lasso* and roped the calf.** (From Spanish *lasso*.) [4]

laugh [laf] *v.* to make special sounds and movements of the face to show one is happy or finds something funny: **We all *laughed* at Rodrigo's joke.** [1]

law·suit [lô′sōōt′] *n.* a court case that makes a civil charge against someone: ***A lawsuit* asks the court to settle a dispute between two sides of an argument.** [8]

leave [lēv] *v.* to cause to be or stay in a certain place: **Please *leave* the book on the table when you're finished.** [2]

lec·ture [lek′chər] *n.* a prepared talk given to an audience, especially a talk by an instructor to an audience of students: **The history professor gave a *lecture* on ancient Egypt. —*v.* to scold in a long, formal way: **If I don't leave now, Dad will *lecture* me about being late.** [10]

lev·el [lev′əl] *n.* the height above sea level: **As the faucet ran, the water *level* in the bathtub rose.** [15]

li·ar [lī′ər] *n.* a person who says something that is not true; a person who tells a lie: **Whoever told you that story must have been a *liar*.** [28]

li·brar·i·an [lī′brâr′ē·ən] *n.* a person who works in a library: **Ask a *librarian* how to find the magazine you want.** [29]

li·brar·y [lī′brâr′ē] *n.* a room or building where a large collection of books is kept: **I borrowed a book about the planets from the *library*.** [35]

life·guard [līf′gârd′] *n.* a person who works at a pool or beach to protect swimmers: **The *lifeguard* gazed out over the water, watching for swimmers in trouble.** [31]

li·on [lī′ən] *n.* a large, powerful animal of the cat family: **You can tell a male *lion* from a female by the male's shaggy mane.** [28]

live [liv] *v.,* **lived, living.** to make one's home: **Our family has *lived* in this house for generations.** [12]

live·stock [līv′stok′] *n.* animals raised on a farm or ranch: **Uncle Ned's *livestock* won several ribbons at the state fair.** [25]

lope [lōp] *v.,* **loped, loping.** to move along easily, with a long, swinging stride: **Our dogs always come *loping* after us when we go for walks.** [3]

lose [lōōz] *v.* to be without something and not know where it is; be unable to find something: **If I *lose* my key, I won't be able to unlock the door.** [3]

love [luv] *v.,* **loved, loving.** to like very, very much: **Katie *loved* this book best of all.** [1]

M

ma·chine [mə·shēn′] *n.* a device made up of parts that act together to do work: **Using a washing *machine* is easier than washing clothes by hand.** [9]

mag·a·zine [mag′ə·zēn′ *or* mag′ə·zēn′] *n.* a collection of articles and stories, often with pictures, usually published weekly or monthly: **Yes, we subscribe to that *magazine*. —*adj.* Mom got the sauce recipe from a *magazine* article about pasta.** [35]

ma·jor leagues [mā′jər lēgz′] *n.* the principal leagues in a professional sport: **The top two teams in the *major leagues* of baseball play in the World Series.** [16]

make·be·lieve [māk′bi·lēv′] *adj.* not real; made up: **Tomás imagined being a pirate on a *make-believe* ship.** *syn.* imaginary [31]

man·u·script [man′yə·skript′] *n.* a typewritten or handwritten copy of a book, article, or other piece of writing, prepared by a writer for typesetting and printing by a publisher: **Keisha sent the *manuscript* of her story to a teen magazine.** [9]

march [märch] *v.,* **marched, marching.** to walk with regular, even steps: **The band *marched* across the football field during halftime.** [8]

marsh [märsh] *n.,* **marshes.** an area of soft, low land that is partly or completely covered by water: **Dragonflies flew among the cattails growing in the soft, wet *marshes*.** [28]

mast [mast] *n.* a long pole that rises straight up from the deck of a ship, used to hold up the sails: **Sailors should know how to climb the ship's *mast*.** [7]

mas·ter·piece [mas′tər·pēs′] *n.* an oustanding work of art: **Grace painted many landscapes, but this one is her *masterpiece*.** [23]

a	add	ō	open	th	thin
ā	ace	ô	order	t͟h	this
â(r)	care	oi	oil	zh	vision
ä	palm	ŏŏ	took		
e	end	ōō	pool	ə	**a** in about
ē	equal	ou	out		**e** in listen
i	it	u	up		**i** in pencil
ī	ice	û(r)	burn		**o** in melon
o	odd	yōō	use		**u** in circus

L
M

may·or [mā′ər] *n.* a person who is elected as the head of a city or town: **Our *mayor* and her council run the town government quite well.** [29]

mea·sure [mezh′ər] *v.* to find or show the size, weight, or amount of something: ***Measure* the flour carefully before putting it into the bowl.** [10]

mem·ber [mem′bər] *n.* a person, animal, or thing that belongs to a certain group: **The *members* of our club all know the secret password.** [25]

mer·chant [mûr′chənt] *n.* a person who owns or is in charge of a store; a person who sells: **Grandma bought these carpets from a traveling rug *merchant*.** [26]

met·al [met′əl] *n.* a hard substance that conducts heat and electricity, and is often made into machine parts: **Most of the plane's instruments were made of *metal*.** [15]

Mex·i·can [mek′sə·kən] *adj.* having to do with Mexico: **Emiliano Zapata was a famous *Mexican* revolutionary leader.** [34]

Mex·i·co [mek′sə·kō′] *n.* a country in southern North America, just south of the United States: **Both *Mexico* and Canada border the United States.** [34]

mi·cro·phone [mī′krə·fōn′] *n.* an instrument that changes sound waves into electrical signals: **Sing into the *microphone* so you can be heard in the back row.** [18]

mi·li·tia [mə·lish′ə] *n.* a group of citizens who are given military training so they can help the armed forces during a war or other emergency: **The *militia* is less experienced than a professional army.** [19]

min·ute [min′it] *n.* a very small amount of time: **It takes just three *minutes* to pop popcorn in the microwave oven.** [27]

mis·er·a·ble [miz′rə·bəl] *adj.* feeling very unhappy; very sad: **Our dog Rover was *miserable* until we washed the skunk smell out of his coat.** [18]

mix·ture [miks′chər] *n.* a combination of two or more components; something mixed together: **A root beer float is a *mixture* of root beer and ice cream.** [10]

mo·bile [mō′bəl] *adj.* able to move or change in position: **Dad had to be *mobile* to work for that company—he was transferred ten times.** [35]

mod·el [mod′əl] *n.* a certain style or type of some manufactured product: **Grandpa likes his old car, but Dad wants a newer *model*.** [15]

moist [moist] *adj.* slightly wet: **The cake is *moist* because I added pudding to the batter.** [6]

mois·ture [mois′chər] *n.* the presence of water or another liquid, especially a small amount of liquid in the air or on a surface: **There's a lot of *moisture* in the air right after a rainstorm.** [10]

mo·ment [mō′mənt] *n.* a very short period of time; an instant: **Take a *moment* to plan before you begin writing.** [27]

mouth [mouth] *n.* the opening in the face through which a person or animal takes in food and drink, and by which sounds are made: **The dentist asked Sarah to open her *mouth*.** [6]

mur·mur [mûr′mər] *v.* to make a soft, low sound that goes on and on: **The audience became impatient and began to *murmur* when the play was late in starting.** [23]

mu·si·cian [myōō·zish′ən] *n.* a person who is good at singing, playing an instrument, or writing music to be played before an audience: **The *musician* practiced every day to prepare for the concert. Every *musician* took part in the performance.** [22, 29]

N

name [nām] *v.,* **named, naming.** to call a person or thing by a certain word or words: **An Indian student *named* Mitu became class president.** [12]

nar·row [nâr′ō] *adj.* not far across; not wide or broad: **That *narrow* street has only one traffic lane.** [25]

na·tion [nā′shən] *n.* a group of people who have a common language, history, and way of life, and who live under one government: **The United States is a *nation* of fifty states.** [19]

nee·dle [nē′dəl] *n.* a long, thin object with a sharp point: **I checked the compass *needle* to make sure we were going west.** [15]

neigh·bor·hood [nā′bər·hŏŏd′] *n.* one particular area within a larger city or town with certain characteristics of its own: **We sometimes eat at a café in our *neighborhood*.** [34]

nine [nīn] *n.* the number that is one more than eight; 9: **Gary is *nine* years old now, but he'll be ten in a week.** [2]

noise [noiz] *n.* a sound that can be heard, especially a loud or disturbing sound: **That's not music; that's *noise*!** [6]

noun [noun] *n.* a word that names a person, place, or thing: **This *noun* is the subject of the sentence.** [6]

oak [ōk] *n.* one of a large group of trees that have acorns: **This strong, tall tree is an *oak*. —*adj*. Each *oak* tree grows from a tiny acorn.** [3]

ob·ject [əb·jekt′] *v.* to be against: **The treasurer will *object* when you ask him to resign.** [25]

o·cean [ō′shən] *n.* the body of salt water that covers about three-fourths of the earth's surface: **Yes, I'd love to swim in the *ocean* again!** [9]

o·dor [ō′dər] *n.* a scent or smell, especially one that is strong or unpleasant: **I knew we were near the seaport when I smelled its fishy** *odor.* [14]

of·fer [ô′fər] *v.* propose as payment: **I'll** *offer* **a reward for the return of my bike.** [7]

of·fice [ôf′is] *n.* a building or other place where the work of a business occurs: **While visiting Mom's** *office,* **I met her secretary.** [25]

of·fi·cer [ôf′ə·sər] *n.* a person who has a certain high rank in the armed forces: **The soldier saluted his commanding** *officer.* [27]

o·pen [ō′pən] *v.,* **opened, opening.** to make or become open: **Gina had been** *opening* **birthday cards when the doorbell rang.** [13]

op·po·si·tion [op′ə·zish′ən] *n.* the act of opposing; being against: **The students spoke in** *opposition* **to canceling summer vacation.** [8]

or·chard [ôr′chərd] *n.* an area of land where fruit trees are grown: **Dad planted more than fifty trees in our apple** *orchard.* [26]

orchard

or·ches·tra [ôr′kəs·trə] *n.* a large group of musicians who all play together on different instruments: *Orchestras* **play different arrangements of this concerto.** [22]

or·der [ôr′dər] *n.* **1.** a direction to do something: **The soldiers obeyed their leader's** *order* **to march forward.** *syn.* command **2.** a certain way that things are arranged: **List your spelling words in alphabetical** *order.* **3.** a situation in which things are arranged or done in the proper way: **The new government restored** *order* **in the country after the war.** —*v.* **1.** to tell someone to do something: **I** *order* **you to be home by nine o'clock! 2.** to ask for; request: **We** *ordered* **flowers for the Thanksgiving dinner table.** [8, 13]

os·trich [os′trich] *n.* a large African bird with long legs and a long neck: **Although the** *ostrich* **is a bird, it can weigh as much as a large man.** [26]

out·doors [out′dôrz′] *adv.* away from houses and other buildings; in the open air: **Let's go** *outdoors* **and slide downhill on our sleds.** [31]

out·field·er [out′fēld′ər] *n.* a player who covers the part of a baseball field beyond the infield: **An** *outfielder* **caught the long fly ball to end the inning.** [16]

ov·en [uv′ən] *n.* an enclosed space, as in a stove, used to heat things placed in it: **Take the pie out of the** *oven* **now or the crust will burn.** [14]

owe [ō] *v.* to have to pay: **I** *owe* **you a dollar, so here it is.** [3]

palm [päm] *n.* the inside of the hand: **Hold out your hand,** *palm* **down.** [33]

pan·o·ram·a [pan′ə·ram′ə] *n.* a wide and complete view of a place: **From the mountaintop Carla looked down and enjoyed the** *panorama* **of the city far below.** [29]

pan·ther [pan′thər] *n.* a name for a large wild cat or leopard, usually with a dark coat: **Though smaller than a lion, a** *panther* **is just as deadly to its prey.** [26]

pas·sen·gers [pas′ən·jərz] *n.* people who ride in a bus, train, airplane, or other vehicle: **Although the train was crowded, all the** *passengers* **found seats.** [33]

pas·ture [pas′chər] *n.* a field or piece of land where farm animals are kept: **Our barn is near the** *pasture* **where the cows are grazing.** [10]

pas·ture·land [pas′chər·land′] *n.* land covered with grass and other growing plants that some farm animals feed on: **You'll need** *pastureland* **for grazing if you buy that herd of cattle.** [25]

pa·ti·o [pat′ē·ō] *n.* an outdoor space next to a house that is usually tiled or paved: **In the summer we often eat breakfast on our sunny** *patio.* (From Spanish *patio.*) [4]

pea·nut [pē′nut′] *n.* a plant seed that grows in pods or shells and develops under the ground: **I cracked the shell and popped one** *peanut* **into my mouth.** [27]

pearl [pûrl] *n.* a small, round, hard object that is formed inside the shell of an oyster: **How can a lowly oyster make such a beautiful** *pearl*? —*adj.* **Mom's** *pearl* **necklace really looks good on you.** [8]

per·cent [pər·sent′] *n.* the number of parts in every hundred: **Carolyn scored 100** *percent* **on the science test.** [9]

per·cus·sion [pər·kush′ən] *adj.* a type of musical instrument that is played by striking or shaking it: **A triangle is a** *percussion* **instrument.** [21]

per·mis·sion [pər·mish′ən] *n.* the fact of being allowed to do something: **Maria needs** *permission* **to leave school early.** *syn.* consent [19]

a	add	ō	open	th	thin
ā	ace	ô	order	t͟h	this
â(r)	care	oi	oil	zh	vision
ä	palm	o͝o	took		
e	end	o͞o	pool	ə	**a** in about
ē	equal	ou	out		**e** in listen
i	it	u	up		**i** in pencil
ī	ice	û(r)	burn		**o** in melon
o	odd	yo͞o	use		**u** in circus

per·mit [pər·mit′] *v.*, **permitted, permitting.** to agree that a person may do something; allow: **Are we *permitted* to start eating before everyone is served?** [13]

per·plexed [pər·plekst′] *adj.* very confused or puzzled: **When his computer didn't work, Nels was totally *perplexed*.** *syn.* baffled [14]

pe·ti·tions [pə·tish′ənz] *n.* formal requests directed to a government or other authority: **In this country the *petitions* of citizens are always heard.** [8]

pi·an·ist [pē·an′ist *or* pē′ə·nist] *n.* a person who plays the piano: **A *pianist* provides background music for our solo singer.** [29]

pi·an·o [pē·an′ō] *n.* a large musical instrument with a keyboard; sound is produced when the keys are pressed, causing felt-covered hammers to strike the metal strings inside: **Both the *piano* and the organ are keyboard instruments.** [21]

pinch hit·ter [pinch′ hit′ər] *n.* in baseball, a player who bats in place of another: **A *pinch hitter* was sent to bat when the bases were loaded.** [16] ◆

◆ **Pinch hitter** comes from the idea that a **pinch** is a tight situation with a lot of pressure. (Think of *pinching* the skin of someone's arm.) A substitute batter in baseball who is sent up to bat late in the game when a hit is badly needed is said to be hitting *in the pinch*. From this came the term *pinch hitter*. Now the term has spread beyond the sport of baseball to mean anyone who substitutes for another person in an important situation: **The mayor was sick, so he sent the deputy mayor to the meeting as his *pinch hitter*.**

pi·o·neer [pī′ə·nir′] *n.* one of the first people to live in a new land or region: **The *pioneer* traveled west from New England by covered wagon.** [29]

plate [plāt] *n.* a dish on which food is placed: **I foolishly filled my *plate* with too much food.** [2]

play [plā] *v.*, **played, playing. 1.** to do something for fun: **We *played* in the yard until it got too dark to see. 2.** to take part in a certain sport or game: **My dad *played* on his college tennis team. 3.** to make music or sound: **Liz always *played* the piano for an hour after school.** [12]

please [plēz] *adv.* a word used to ask for something in a polite way: ***Please* return my book when you've finished reading it.** [9]

pleased [plēzd] *adj.* feeling good about something: **Mom is *pleased* that I cleaned my room without being told.** [12]

pleas·ure [plezh′ər] *n.* the feeling of liking something; a feeling of being happy or enjoying something: **It was a real *pleasure* to meet you, Mr. President!** [10]

po·em [pō′əm] *n.* a form of writing in which sound, rhythm, and meaning combine to create ideas and feelings: **A sonnet is a *poem* with fourteen lines and a special pattern of rhyme.** [28]

po·et [pō′it] *n.* a person who writes poems: **Which American *poet* wrote "Annabel Lee"?** [28]

po·lite [pə·līt′] *adj.* having or showing good manners: **It's *polite* to ask for an apple before taking one.** *syn.* courteous [6]

pop·u·lar [pop′yə·lər] *adj.* well liked; approved of by many people: **Theo is so *popular* that I don't know anyone who dislikes him.** [32]

pop·u·la·tion [pop′yə·lā′shən] *n.* the total number of people who live in a place, or these people as a group: **Our town's *population* is growing fast, as new families move here.** [32]

porch [pôrch] *n.* a covered entrance attached to a house: **On summer evenings we often relax on our *porch*.** [8]

por·ter [pôr′tər] *n.* someone who assists passengers, usually on a train: **Dad gave the *porter* a tip for carrying our suitcases.** [33]

por·trait [pôr′trit *or* pôr′trāt′] *n.* a formal painting or photograph of a person or a group: **We've wanted a family *portrait*, so we finally had one taken.** [26]

po·ta·to [pə·tā′tō] *n.* a round or oval-shaped vegetable that grows under the ground: **One large *potato* makes a lot of french fries.** (From Spanish *patata*.) [4]

prac·ti·cal [prak′ti·kəl] *adj.* suited for actual use; useful: **Lace isn't a *practical* fabric for a kitchen.** [26]

prac·tice [prak′tis] *n.* the act or fact of doing something over and over: **The basketball team could use some extra *practice*.** —*v.*, **practiced, practicing.** to do something over and over to get better at it: **That screeching tells me that Matt is *practicing* the violin.** [9, 12]

pre·cau·tion [pri·kô′shən] *n.* something done ahead of time to prevent danger or harm: **When you leave home, follow every safety *precaution* you know.** [20]

pre·dict [pri·dikt′] *v.* to say ahead of time that something will happen in a certain way: **If I could *predict* the future, I'd know what will happen next year.** [20]

pre·fer [pri·fûr′] *v.* to like one thing better than another: **I *prefer* to sit at the front of the theater.** [20]

pre·pare [pri·pâr′] *v.*, **prepared, preparing.** to make or become ready: **Paula *prepared* for the recital by practicing every day.** [20]

pres·ent [prez′ənt] *adj.* going on now: **At the *present* time, you're doing very well in math.** [9]

pres·sure [presh′ər] *n.* strong influence or persuasion to do something: **The mayor is under *pressure* from the voters to save Midtown Park from being sold.** [9]

pre·tend [pri·tend′] *v.*, **pretended, pretending.** to act as if something is true or real when it is not; make believe: **The children *pretended* to be invisible.** [20]

pre·vent [pri·vent′] *v.* to keep something from happening: **You can help *prevent* forest fires by not using matches here.** [20]

pre·view [prē′vyōō′] *n.* a showing of something before its regular opening: **Ruth saw a short *preview* of next weekend's movie.** —*v.* to show something before its regular opening: **The director will *preview* her film before it is released.** [20]

pre·vi·ous [prē′vē·əs] *adj.* coming before something else: **I saw this exhibit on a *previous* trip to the museum.** *syn.* earlier [20]

pri·or [prī′ər] *adj.* former; earlier: **Both this and my *prior* report card were good.** [28]

pri·vate [prī′vit] *adj.* not meant to be shared with others; personal: **Get a *private* room if you don't want a roommate.** [27]

prob·a·ble [prob′ə·bəl] *adj.* fairly certain to happen or be true: **It's *probable* that the kitten jumped out when you opened the window.** [18]

prob·a·bly [prob′ə·blē *or* prob′lē] *adv.* almost certainly or definitely: **It will *probably* be sunny, but there's a slight chance of rain.** [35]

pro·cess [pros′es] *n.* a series of actions to make or do something: **Do you know the *process* used for recycling paper?** —*v.* to prepare or do something using a series of steps: **Our secretary will *process* the job applications.** [20]

pro·duce [prə·dōōs′] *v.* to grow, make, or build something: **Ohio and Indiana both *produce* large corn crops.** [20]

pro·duc·er [prə·dōō′sər] *n.* a person in charge of bringing a play, movie, or the like before the public: **Tracy was both star and *producer* of the video.** [18]

prod·uct [prod′ukt] *n.* anything that is made or manufactured: **Milk is the main *product* of a dairy farm.** [20]

pro·gram [prō′gram′] *n.* a meeting, performance, or other such activity: **Our music *program* will begin with a piano solo.** [20]

proj·ect [proj′ekt] *n.* a plan or effort to carry out some task: **Chi Wan's first woodworking *project* was a pine bookshelf.** —*v.* **pro·ject** [prə·jekt′] to cause something to be displayed or visible over a distance: **Please *project* the slides on the back wall.** [20]

prom·ise [prom′is] *v.,* promised, promising. to state that one will surely do something or that something will surely happen: **Consuelo can't go bowling because she *promised* to baby-sit for her little brother.** [20]

pro·tect [prō·tekt′] *v.* to keep or guard from harm or danger: **The lioness will *protect* her cubs from harm.** *syn.* defend [20]

proud [proud] *adj.* feeling happy about something good that you or somebody else has done: **I'm *proud* of Amrita for winning the tennis tournament.** [6]

prove [prōōv] *v.* to show that something is true: **The lawyer will *prove* that Brian didn't steal anything.** [3]

pro·vide [prə·vīd′] *v.* to give what is needed or wanted: **We'll *provide* food for the party if you'll bring the sodas.** [20]

pub·lish·er [pub′lish·ər] *n.* a person or company that produces newspapers, magazines, or books for sale to the public: **The *publisher* is happy with the sales of Mr. Arnaud's book.** [9]

pur·chase [pûr′chəs] *v.* to get something by paying money: **My Aunt Pilar will *purchase* a car when next year's models come out.** [26]

Q

quart·er [kwôr′tər] *adj.* being one of four equal parts; one-fourth: **Each college year is made up of four *quarter* sessions.** [8]

ques·tion [kwes′chən] *n.* something asked to find out information; something that calls for an answer: **Raise your hand if you have a *question*.** [19]

qui·et [kwī′ət] *adj.* with little or no noise: **The house was so *quiet* that I could hear the clock ticking.** [28]

quit [kwit] *v.* to stop doing something: **Luis had to *quit* his job when he started playing on the football team.** [1]

R

rail·road [rāl′rōd′] *n.* a transportation system in which people and goods are moved by train along a track made of metal rails. *Railroads* provide reliable transportation for people and freight. [33]

ram·parts [ram′pärts] *n.* earth embankments around a castle, fort, or the like, for defense against attack: **The *ramparts* surrounding the fort protected it from attack.** [19]

a	add	ō	open	th	thin
ā	ace	ô	order	th	this
â(r)	care	oi	oil	zh	vision
ä	palm	ŏŏ	took		
e	end	ōō	pool	ə	**a** in about
ē	equal	ou	out		**e** in listen
i	it	u	up		**i** in pencil
ī	ice	û(r)	burn		**o** in melon
o	odd	yōō	use		**u** in circus

rath·er [rath´ər] *adv.* more willing to do one thing than another: **Would you *rather* walk to school or take the bus?** [14]

rat·tle [rat´əl] *v.* to make a series of short, sharp sounds: **Our windows sometimes *rattle* during thunderstorms.** —*n.* an object that makes short, sharp sounds such as a toy: **The baby likes to make noise by shaking his *rattle*.** [23]

rat·tle·snake [rat´əl·snāk´] *n.* a poisonous American snake: **A *rattlesnake* that shakes its tail may be preparing to strike.** [31]

ray [rā] *n.* a narrow beam of light: **A *ray* of sun broke though the clouds.** [2]

re·act [rē·akt´] *v.* to act in response to something that has happened: **I *react* to problems by trying to solve them.** [28]

rea·son·a·ble [rēz´nə·bel *or* rēz´ən·ə·bəl] *adj.* showing good sense: **"I'm sorry, but that's not a *reasonable* request," said the librarian.** [18]

re·ceive [ri·sēv´] *v.* to get or take what is given: **You'll *receive* your new library card in the mail.** [32]

re·cep·tion [ri·sep´shən] *n.* **1.** welcome: **We gave the new teacher a warm *reception*. 2.** a party or social gathering to welcome guests: **The principal will host an afternoon *reception* for parents of the new fifth-graders.** —*adj.* **This wedding has a very long *reception* line.** [32]

re·cit·al [ri·sī´təl] *n.* a public concert or performance: **My partner and I will sing a duet for the *recital*.** [21]

re·cy·cle [rē·sī´kəl] *v.* to prepare or treat something so that it can be used again, and not be thrown away: **We save paper, glass, and plastic to *recycle* them.** [35]

glass   papers   cans

recycle

re·fer [ri·fûr´] *v.,* **referred, referring. 1.** to call by a certain name: **Now that she's an American citizen, Han-Ling wants to be *referred* to as Helen. 2.** to send or direct a person somewhere else for help or information: **The librarian *referred* me to the young adult section.** [13]

re·fuse [ri·fyooz´] *v.,* **refused, refusing.** to decide not to do or allow something: **I *refused* to accept the award because I didn't think I deserved it.** [9]

re·gret [ri·gret´] *v.,* **regretted, regretting.** to feel sorry about something: **Bob *regretted* his part in the practical joke.** [13]

re·hearse [ri·hûrs´] *v.* to practice or train before performing: **If Kachina *rehearses* often enough, she'll be ready for opening night.** [21]

reign [rān] *v.* to be everywhere; prevail: **Dad says "Let silence *reign*!" when he means "Be quiet!"** [33]

re·lax [ri·laks´] *v.* to take it easy without worry: **After dinner, Dad likes to *relax* in his favorite chair.** [21]

re·lo·cate [rē·lō´kāt] *v.* to move to a new location: **We'll *relocate* from New York to California within six weeks.** [35]

re·mark·a·ble [ri·mär´kə·bəl] *adj.* worth being noticed or spoken about; very unusual: **Her quick recovery from the accident was certainly *remarkable*.** [18]

re·mem·ber [ri·mem´bər] *v.,* **remembered, remembering.** to think of again; bring back to mind: **Even little Tommy *remembered* seeing the Statue of Liberty.** [13]

re·mind [ri·mīnd´] *v.* to cause a person to remember something: **Please *remind* me to return my library book when it's due.** [21]

rem·i·nisce [rem´ə·nis´] *v.,* **reminisced, reminiscing.** to think or tell about past experiences: **Mom and I were *reminiscing* about the day we adopted our first cat.** [13]

re·pair [ri·pâr´] *v.* to change something that is broken or not working so that it is back in good condition: **When our car breaks down, Mom can sometimes *repair* it herself.** *syn.* fix [8]

re·signed [ri·zīnd´] *adj.* accepting problems or difficulties patiently, without complaint: ***Resigned* to walking home, Ken was grateful that Diego offered him a ride.** [13]

re·spect·ful [ri·spekt´fəl] *adj.* having or showing care for: **Being *respectful* of the land means not wasting its resources.** [26]

re·spon·si·ble [ri·spon´sə·bəl] *adj.* being the cause of something; being accountable for one's actions: **Who's *responsible* for making this mess?** [18]

re·tri·al [rē´trī´əl] *n.* the process of hearing and judging evidence a second time in a court of law, to determine whether a new verdict should be made: **The lawyer demanded a *retrial* for his client.** [8]

re·turn [ri·tûrn´] *v.* to come or go back: **We'll leave in the morning and *return* before dark.** [21]

re·view [ri·vyoo´] *v.* to look over or study again: **We'll *review* the lesson as we study for our test.** [21]

rhythm [ri´thəm] *n.* the repetition of sounds or movements in a certain pattern: **We tapped our feet to the *rhythm* of the music.** [20]

rig·ging [rig´ing] *n.* the ropes or cables that hold the sails on a ship: **The sailor climbed up the ship's *rigging* to see if land was near.** [7]

ri·ot [rī´ət] *n.* a violent, noisy disturbance: **Please don't start a *riot* in my hometown.** —*v.* to create a violent, noisy disturbance: **The workers will *riot* if their demands aren't met.** [28]

roar [rôr] *v.*, **roared, roaring.** to make a very loud, deep noise: **One lion was** *roaring* **during the circus act.** [23]

rob·in [rob′ən] *n.* a bird that lives in North America and Europe: **The** *robin* **puffed up its red breast and tugged at the worm.** [27]

ro·de·o [ro′dē·o *or* ro·dā′ō] *n.* a show with contests in the skills that a cowhand of the Old West had to have, such as horseback riding, roping, and steer wrestling: **A** *rodeo* **may seem exciting, but it's no fun for the animals.** [4] ◆

◆ **Rodeo** comes from the Spanish word *rodear,* meaning "to surround." The first meaning of the word *rodeo* was "a roundup of cattle." The Spanish were the first cowhands in the American West, and many of the English words that have to do with their lives come from Spanish. Other such words besides *rodeo* include *lariat, lasso, ranch, chaps,* and *stampede.*

rook·ie [rŏŏk′ē] *n.* someone who is new at something or who has very little experience: **A** *rookie* **led the league in stolen bases this year.** [29]

round [round] *adj.* shaped like a ball or globe: **The planet Earth is** *round.* [6]

ru·in [rōō′ən] *v.* to cause great damage; harm greatly: **You'll** *ruin* **your teeth if you don't brush and floss every day.** *syns.* spoil, destroy —*n.* what is left of something that has been destroyed; remains: **Those** *ruins* **were once the temple of Athena.** [28]

rule [rōōl] *n.* a guide or condition that controls how something is done: **The most important** *rule* **for our game is that no one can cheat.** —*v.* to govern or have control over: **To** *rule* **well, a leader must be fair.** [3]

rus·tle [rus′əl] *v.*, **rustled, rustling.** to make a soft, fluttering sound: **The leaves were** *rustling* **in the wind.** [23]

say [sā] *v.*, **says, said, saying.** to speak words out loud: **The coach** *says* **that our team will play well in the game if we practice hard this week.** [1]

scen·er·y [sēn′rē *or* sē′nər·ē] *n.* the way a place looks, especially an outdoor place; a beautiful landscape: **Brightly colored trees make New England's** *scenery* **spectacular in fall.** [29]

sci·ence [sī′əns] *n.* the careful study of the world to learn the facts about it: **Chemistry and biology are two branches of** *science.* [28]

sci·en·tist [sī′ən·tist] *n.* a person who works in one of the fields of science: **That** *scientist* **does not experiment on animals.** [29]

sculp·ture [skulp′chər] *n.* a figure or design made from clay, stone, wood, or metal: **Although he's blind, Jake can "see" a** *sculpture* **by touching it.** [10]

sec·tion [sek′shən] *n.* one part of a whole thing: **The first** *section* **of Roberto's essay was an introduction.** [19]

sen·si·ble [sen′sə·bəl] *adj.* showing good judgment: **It's** *sensible* **to take a nap now so you can stay up later.** *syn.* reasonable [18]

sen·tence [sen′təns] *n.* a group of words that expresses a complete thought: **Write a** *sentence* **using the new verb you learned today.** [9]

set·tlers [set′lərz] *n.* people who go to live in a new area or country, especially those among the first to live there: **The** *settlers* **riding westward faced all kinds of problems.** [32]

sev·en·ty-five [sev′ən·tē-fīv′] *adj.* five more than seventy; 75: **My lemonade cost** *seventy-five* **cents.** [31]

shark [shärk] *n.* a meat-eating fish that lives in oceans throughout the world: **The beach was closed because a** *shark* **was seen near shore.** [8]

ship·board [ship′bôrd′] *n.* on a ship: **If you take a cruise, you spend most of your time on** *shipboard.* [12]

shoe·mak·er [shōō′mā′kər] *n.* a person whose work is making or repairing shoes: **Our** *shoemaker* **can actually make old shoes look new.** [10]

shoot [shōōt] *v.*, **shot, shooting.** to fire a gun or other firearm: **The sheriff** *shot* **the outlaw in the arm during a gunfight.** [1]

shot [shot] *n.* **1.** the act of firing a gun: **The police officer fired a warning** *shot* **when he saw the prisoner escaping. 2.** an injection of medicine given with a needle: **Dr. Jenkins gave me a penicillin** *shot* **when I was sick.** [1]

should [shŏŏd] *v.* a verb used with other verbs to show a need to do something: **Dad says I** *should* **finish dinner before asking for dessert.** [7]

show·er [shou′ər] *n.* **1.** a short rainfall: **The sun came out again after the rain** *shower.* **2.** a party at which a woman's friends give her gifts to celebrate a happy event: **Anne and I were invited to Amanda's wedding** *shower.* —*v.* to bathe in water that sprays down from

a	add	ō	open	th	thin
ā	ace	ô	order	th	this
â(r)	care	oi	oil	zh	vision
ä	palm	ŏŏ	took		
e	end	ōō	pool	ə	**a** in about
ē	equal	ou	out		**e** in listen
i	it	u	up		**i** in pencil
ī	ice	û(r)	burn		**o** in melon
o	odd	yōō	use		**u** in circus

above: **I *shower* first in the morning, so I always have enough hot water.** [6]

si·lo [sī′lō] *n.* a tall, round building used for storing food for farm animals: **We harvest our grain and then store it in the *silo*.** [25]

sil·ver·smith [sil′vər·smith′] *n.* a person who makes things of silver or repairs silver: **Great-grandma's silver teapot was made by a *silversmith* in Maine.** [10]

sim·ple [sim′pəl] *adj.* not hard to understand or do; not difficult: **The *simple* recipe had only three steps.** [15]

sin·gle [sing′gəl] *adj.* not married: **Mom and Dad were *single* people before they got married.** [15]

siz·zle [siz′əl] *v.* to make a hissing or crackling sound: **Keep those hot dogs on the grill until they *sizzle*.** [23]

slight [slīt] *adj.* small in amount, size, degree, or importance: **Sarah has only a *slight* cold, so she should feel better soon.** [2]

slink [slingk] *v.,* slunk, slinking. to move in a quiet, sneaking way: **Mom scolded our dog for barking, and now he's *slinking* away to hide.** [3]

slurp [slûrp] *v.* to eat or drink in a noisy manner: **It's not polite to *slurp* while you're eating.** [23]

smart [smärt] *adj.* having a good mind: **Grandpa is *smart*; he can figure out the answers to many problems.** *syn.* intelligent [8]

smoke·stack [smōk′stak′] *n.* a large chimney for carrying away smoke from a furnace or engine: **Thick smoke rose from the ship's *smokestack*.** [12]

sol·dier [sōl′jər] *n.* a person who serves in the army, especially one who is not an officer: **Patrick enlisted in the army because he wanted to be a *soldier*.** [27]

sol·emn·ly [sol′əm·lē] *adv.* seriously; gravely: **The witness promised *solemnly* to tell the truth.** [13]

sol·id [sol′əd] *adj.* 1. having a definite shape and firmness; not a liquid or gas: **Cement is *solid* when it dries.** 2. made of one material: **This *solid* gold ring bends easily.** 3. without breaks; entire: **Jorge's argument is *solid* because he backs it up with facts.** [27]

so·pran·o [sə·pran′ō] *n.,* sopranos. the highest singing voice for women, or a person who has such a voice: ***Sopranos* have the highest voices of all the choir members.** [22]

soul [sōl] *n.* a person's being or existence: **Uncle Ned is afraid of water and won't swim to save his *soul*.** [3]

sound [sound] *n.* something that can be heard; a certain noise: **Is that the *sound* of thunder?** [6]

space [spās] *n.* any area that has limits: **I have plenty of closet *space* for storing our winter coats.** [2]

spare [spâr] *v.* to keep from being hurt or punished: **Take Sam out of the game to *spare* him further pain.** [8]

splash [splash] *v.* to cause water or other liquids to fly about: **Let's *splash* some ice water on the fresh fruit.** [23]

spoil [spoil] *v.* 1. to hurt or ruin in some way: **We'll *spoil* the painting if we touch it before it's dry. 2.** to become decayed or rotten: **That meat will *spoil* unless you keep it in the refrigerator. 3.** to allow a person, especially a child, to become selfish because of easy treatment: **You'll *spoil* the baby if you let him have his way all the time.** [6]

squawk [skwôk] *v.,* squawked, squawking. to make a loud, shrill cry: **The parrot *squawked* and said "Gimme five!"** [23]

squeak [skwēk] *v.* to make a short, sharp, high sound: **Did the mouse *squeak* before it ran away?** [23]

stam·pede [stam·ped′] *n.* a sudden, wild movement of animals or people in a group: **The cattle *stampede* began when that rifle shot rang out.** (From Spanish *estampida*, "uproar.") [4]

sta·tion [stā′shən] *n.* a person's place in society: **A king's *station* in life is higher than that of his people.** [9]

steal [stēl] *v.,* stole, stolen, stealing. to take property that belongs to another without right or permission: **The police never found the money that was *stolen* in that bank robbery.** [27]

straight [strāt] *adj.* not curved; going in an even way in one direction: **Julia has *straight* blond hair.** —*adv.* without delay or interruption: **Go *straight* home from school.** [2]

struc·ture [struk′chər] *n.* something that is built: **A house is a simpler *structure* than a skyscraper.** [10]

stu·di·o [stoo′dē·ō] *n.* a place where movies are filmed or radio and television programs are made: **The television *studio* is already full.** —*adj.* **The *studio* audience cheered when the star appeared.** [18]

style [stīl] *n.* qualities that make something distinct and different from others: **You have a pleasing writing *style*.** [2]

sub·sti·tute [sub′stə·toot′] *v.* to replace something with another: **You may *substitute* margarine for butter in this recipe.** —*adj.* used in place of another: **The *substitute* goalie played very well.** [35]

sud·den·ly [sud′ən·lē] *adv.* happening quickly and without warning: ***Suddenly* the horse reared and threw me out of the saddle.** [35]

suf·fer [suf′ər] *v.,* suffered, suffering. to feel pain or sadness: **Ramón *suffered* from headaches until he finally went to the doctor.** [13]

suit [soot] *v.* to be right for or meet the needs of: **Perfume doesn't *suit* Grandma, so I bought her a photo album instead.** [3]

suit·a·ble [soot′ə·bəl] *adj.* right for a certain purpose: **Sandals aren't *suitable* to wear in the snow.** [18]

sup·port [sə·pôrt′] *n.* the act of assisting or helping: **True friends give each other *support* in times of trouble.** [25]

S

sup·pose [sə·pōz'] *v.*, **supposed, supposing. 1.** imagine or think possible; believe: **I** *suppose* **that George has written another letter to the editor. 2.** expected: **I'm** *supposed* **to wash my hands before dinner.** [12]

sure [sho͝or] *adj.* having no doubt about: **Be** *sure* **you turn off the oven when the meatloaf is done.** [9]

sur·prised [sə·prīzd' *or* sər·prīzd'] *adj.* feeling wonder or amazement caused by something unexpected: **Mom was** *surprised* **when she received roses on her birthday.** [12]

sur·vive [sûr·vīv'] *v.* to stay alive: **The wilting plant will** *survive* **if we give it water.** [25]

switch [swich] *n.* a device for breaking an electrical circuit: **Flip the** *switch* **and the light will come on.** [1]

sword [sôrd] *n.* a weapon having a long, sharp blade set in a handle or hilt: **The duel began when each actor picked up a** *sword.* [33]

T

tall [tôl] *adj.* higher than average; not short: **Today, basketball is a sport for very** *tall* **players.** [7]

teach [tēch] *v.*, **taught, teaching. 1.** to give knowledge to; cause to learn: **Mr. Brewster** *teaches* **us spelling every morning. 2.** to give lessons as one's job; work as a teacher in school: **My first-grade teacher** *taught* **for forty years before she retired. Mrs. Espinoza has been** *teaching* **at our school for ten years.** [7, 12]

teach·ing [tē'ching] *n.* the act or fact of giving instruction to students: *Teaching* **is a rewarding career.** [12]

tease [tēz] *v.* to annoy someone in a playful way: **Don't** *tease* **the baby or he'll begin to cry.** [2]

tel·e·vi·sion [tel'ə·vizh'ən] *n.* a system of sending pictures and sounds through the air electronically: **We watch the news on** *television* **at six o'clock every night.** —*adj.* **The** *television* **repair shop has an assortment of electronic gear.** [19]

ten·nis [ten'is] *n.* a game in which two or four players use racquets to hit a ball over a net: **You can't play** *tennis* **without a racquet.** [25]

ten·or [ten'ər] *n.* the highest adult male singing voice, or a singer who has this voice: **Many famous male opera singers are** *tenors.* [22]

ter·ri·ble [ter'ə·bəl] *adj.* very bad or unpleasant: **That** *terrible* **storm caused a great deal of damage.** [18]

ter·ror [ter'ər] *n.* very great fear: **Ellen loved the raft trip, but Don remembered it with** *terror.* [14]

Thanks·giv·ing [thangks'giv'ing] *n.* a national holiday in which people give thanks by feasting and prayer: **I never get tired of celebrating** *Thanksgiving* **with my family.** [31]

theirs [t͟hârz] *pron.* belonging to them: **These seats are ours, and the ones in the next row are** *theirs.* [16]

there's [t͟hârz] *cont.* a short form for *there is:* **"***There's* **a new CD I'd like to hear," said Ruma.** [16]

think [thingk] *v.*, **thought, thinking.** to suppose: **I** *thought* **Rick would know the answer because he's very smart.** [7]

thought [thôt] *n.* the result of thinking; an idea or opinion: **When the fire broke out, his first** *thought* **was to get out of the house.** —*v.* the past form of **think. Rafael** *thought* **that the math test was easy.** [7]

throat [thrōt] *n.* the passage from the mouth to the stomach: **It hurts when I swallow food because I have a sore** *throat.* [3]

to·ma·to [tə·mā'tō *or* tə·mä'tō] *n.* a plump, juicy, red or yellow fruit with seeds and a smooth skin, widely used as a vegetable: **Jan eats a** *tomato* **every day just for the vitamins it contains.** —*adj.* **Those ripe** *tomato* **wedges really brighten up your salad.** (From Spanish *tomate.*) [4]

tor·na·do [tôr·nā'dō] *n.* a violent windstorm that creates a dark, twisting, funnel-shaped cloud: **A** *tornado* **usually appears as a funnel-shaped cloud.** (From Spanish *tornado,* "thunderstorm.") [4]

tour·ist [to͝or'ist] *n.* a person who travels to visit a place for pleasure: **The** *tourist* **spoke enough French to find her way around Paris.** [29]

tow·er [tou'ər] *n.* a high, often narrow structure that stands alone or is part of a larger building: **The bells chimed in the church** *tower.* [14]

town [toun] *n.* an area with many houses and other buildings in which people live and work: **I still live in the** *town* **where I was born.** [6]

trail [trāl] *v.* to follow the tracks or path of: **There's Pete's beagle,** *trailing* **along after him as usual.** [3]

trans·port [trans·pôrt'] *v.* to bring or carry someone or something from one place to another: **The plane will** *transport* **us across the Pacific Ocean to Hawaii.** [35]

trav·el [trav'əl] *v.* to go from one place to another: **How long does it take to** *travel* **to Raleigh from Goldsboro?** [27]

trav·el·er [tra'və·lər] *n.* a person who goes from one place to another for business or pleasure: **An experienced** *traveler* **can pack a suitcase well.** [35]

a	add	ō	open	th	thin
ā	ace	ô	order	t͟h	this
â(r)	care	oi	oil	zh	vision
ä	palm	o͝o	took		
e	end	ō͞o	pool	ə	**a** in about
ē	equal	ou	out		**e** in listen
i	it	u	up		**i** in pencil
ī	ice	û(r)	burn		**o** in melon
o	odd	yō͞o	use		**u** in circus

trea·sure [trezh′ər] *n.* great wealth, especially money or jewelry that has been stored away or hidden: **Do you enjoy books about buried** *treasure?* [10]

tri·al [trī′əl] *n.* **1.** the process of determining in a court of law whether a charge or accusation is true: **At the** *trial* **the jury sat quietly, listening carefully. 2.** a test of patience or strength: **Michiko sighed, "Caring for a baby brother is a real** *trial.*" —*adj.* done as a test or experiment: **"I'll do a** *trial* **run first to check the track," said Mrs. Petrakis.** [15]

trick·le [trik′əl] *v.,* **trickled, trickling.** to fall in drops or in a slow, thin stream: **Water** *trickled* **from the faucet until we had it repaired.** [23]

trig·gered [trig′ərd] *adj.* set to act like a trigger in causing or starting something: **The alarm, already** *triggered,* **went off when the window was opened.** [1]

tri·umph [trī′əmf] *n.* something that is gained or won after a struggle: **One of Jackie Joyner-Kersee's greatest** *triumphs* **was winning an Olympic medal.** *syn.* victory [28]

troop [troop] *n.* a group of people who fight on the same side in a war: **The** *troop* **of soldiers shared both tents and food.** [27]

true [troo] *adj.* agreeing with the facts: **It's** *true* **that a right angle has ninety degrees.** [3]

tu·na [too′nə] *n.* any of several kinds of large saltwater fish found in warm seas: **I don't like fish as a rule, but I do like** *tuna.* (From Spanish *atún.*) [4]

tun·dra [tun′drə] *n.* a wide plain above the tree line, found in Arctic regions: **A** *tundra* **stays frozen all year long.** [28]

tundra

turn [tûrn] *v.,* **turned, turning.** to change the condition or form of: **Soon the tadpole had** *turned* **into a frog.** [12]

twirl [twûrl] *v.* to spin or wind around: **Jenny will** *twirl* **a baton in the Fourth of July parade.** [8]

um·pire [um′pīr′] *n.* a person who rules on plays in baseball and other sports: **The** *umpire* **cried "Strike three!" and the batter was out.** [16]

un·cov·er [ən·kuv′ər] *v.* **1.** to discover and make known: **The detective may** *uncover* **the crooks' plan and solve the crime. 2.** to take off a cover: **Don't** *uncover* **the pot until the beans are done.** [21]

un·eas·y [ən·ē′zē] *adj.* nervous; worried: **Standing by the edge of the cliff made me** *uneasy.* [21]

u·nit·ed [yoo·nī′tid] *adj.* joined together; making up a unit: **Our** *united* **voices give the chorus a special sound.** [32]

u·ni·ty [yoo′nə·tē] *n.* the fact of being united: **In a rare display of** *unity,* **the senators approved the budget.** [32]

un·known [ən·nōn′] *adj.* not discovered; not known: **The unsigned note was written by someone** *unknown.* [21]

un·pleas·ant [ən·plez′ənt] *adj.* not agreeable: **Picking up spilled garbage is an** *unpleasant* **task.** [21]

up·stairs [up′stârz′] *adv.* up the stairs or to an upper floor: **Let's go** *upstairs* **and rummage around in the attic.** —*adj.* located on a higher floor: **The** *upstairs* **apartment has just been rented.** [31]

va·cant [vā′kənt] *adj.* not occupied: **That lot was** *vacant* **until the city built a library on it.** *syn.* empty [27]

va·ca·tion [vā·kā′shən] *n.* a period of time spent away from school or work: **This year we're spending our summer** *vacation* **at home.** [19]

val·u·a·ble [val′yə·bəl] *adj.* very important or useful: **Gold is a** *valuable* **metal.** [18]

va·nil·la [və·nel′ə *or* və·nil′ə] *n.* a flavoring made from the dried seed pods of a certain tropical plant. **Dad used** *vanilla* **to flavor the pudding.** —*adj.* flavored with or made from vanilla: **I'll have two scoops of** *vanilla* **ice cream for dessert.** (From Spanish *vainilla,* "small sheath.") [4]

vanilla

vi·cin·i·ty [və·sin′ə·tē] *n.* the area around or near a particular place: **Shopping is easy because we live in the** *vicinity* **of the mall.** [34]

Vi·et·nam [vē′et·näm′] *n.* a country in southeast Asia: **Hanoi, the capital of** *Vietnam,* **is in the northern part of the country.** [34]

Vi·et·nam·ese [vē·et′nə·mēz′] *adj.* having to do with the people or culture of Vietnam: **Ho Chi Minh was a** *Vietnamese* **Communist leader.** [34]

vi·o·lin [vī′ə·lin′] *n.* a musical instrument with a wooden body, played by drawing a bow across four strings: **The** *violin* **is one of the instruments in a string quartet.** [20]

vis·i·ble [viz′ə·bəl] *adj.* able to be seen: **The North Star is** *visible* **on clear nights.** [18]

vis·it [viz′ət] *v.*, **visited, visiting.** to go to see a person or a place for a period of time: **Grandma sleeps in my bedroom while she is** *visiting* **us.** [13]

vis·ta [vis′tə] *n.* a view, especially one seen from afar: **The** *vista* **from the rim of the canyon is awesome.** [29]

vol·ca·no [vol·kā′nō] *n.* an opening in the earth's crust through which lava, hot gases, ashes, and pieces of rock burst: **As the** *volcano* **erupted, smoke and lava poured forth.** [35]

voy·age [voi′ij] *n.* a trip or journey, especially a long trip over water: **Greta arrived here after a long** *voyage* **across the Atlantic Ocean.** [7]

walk [wôk] *v.*, **walked, walking.** to move on foot at a normal rate: **As we were** *walking* **along, Hale suddenly tripped and fell.** [12]

warn [wôrn] *v.* to give notice of possible harm or danger: **The weather forecasters will** *warn* **us when a storm is on the way.** [8]

watch [wäch] *v.*, **watched, watching.** to look at; sense with the eyes: **I always** *watch* **for the first flowers to bloom. Liza** *watched* **the lightning flash.** [1, 12]

wel·come [wel′kəm] *v.* to greet in a friendly way: **We'll** *welcome* **the new students and make them feel at home.** [25]

who's [hōoz] *cont.* a shortened form of *who is* and *who has*: *Who's* **that on the phone?** [16]

whose [hōoz] *pron.* the possessive form of *who* or *which*: *Whose* **turn is it to go next?** [16]

wil·der·ness [wil′dər·nis] *n.* an area in which plants grow wild and in which few or no people live: **The house was in the** *wilderness,* **hundreds of miles from any town.** [32]

win·dow [win′dō] *n.* an opening in a wall that lets in light and air: **I pushed the curtain aside and looked out the** *window.* [25]

wis·dom [wiz′dəm] *n.* the ability to judge what is right, based on intelligence and experience: **Grandpa's** *wisdom* **comes from many years of living.** [32]

wise [wīz] *adj.* showing the ability to understand and make the right decisions; sensible: **Your decision not to skate on thin ice was a** *wise* **one.** [32]

wolf [woŏlf] *n.* a large, powerful wild member of the dog family: **The** *wolf* **ran off into the woods.** [7]

wom·an [woŏm′ən] *n.* a full-grown female person: **No** *woman* **has yet been elected as President of the United States.** [14]

won·der [wun′dər] *v.*, **wondered, wondering.** to want to know about: **We're** *wondering* **whether you'd like to join our volleyball team.** [13]

wood·wind [woŏd′wind′] *n.* a musical instrument, originally made of wood, that makes a sound when air is blown through the mouthpiece: **A clarinet is a** *woodwind.* **—adj. Aaron plays his clarinet in the** *woodwind* **section of the orchestra.** [21]

would [woŏd] *v.* a polite word to use in a request or question: *Would* **you like help with your homework?** [33]

wrap [rap] *v.* to wind or fold about something: *Wrap* **a napkin around the cookies and take them home.** [33]

wreck [rek] *n.* the damaging or destroying of a car, train, or other vehicle when it strikes heavily against another object: **Dad wasn't hurt in the** *wreck,* **thank goodness.** [33]

wrin·kle [ring′kəl] *v.*, **wrinkled, wrinkling.** to form small ridges or creases in a smooth surface, such as cloth or skin: **The rabbit's whiskers twitched when it** *wrinkled* **its nose.** [33]

write [rīt] *v.*, **wrote, written, writing. 1.** to form letters or words on paper or another such surface: **Mrs. Lorenson was** *writing* **on the board when Annie came in. 2.** to create a poem, story, play, article, or the like: **I've started to** *write* **my autobiography in case I become famous someday.** [12]

writ·ing [rīt′ing] *n.* **1.** something written: **Marvin sent me a letter, but I can't read his** *writing.* **2.** the act of creating poems, stories, or plays as a job: *Writing* **is a wonderful career if readers like your work.** [12]

year [yēr] *n.* a period of twelve months, or 365 days: **Grandma is fifty** *years* **older than I am.** [9]

yolk [yōk] *n.* the yellow part of an egg: **I won't eat a fried egg if the** *yolk* **is runny.** [33]

a	add	ō	open	th	thin
ā	ace	ô	order	th	this
â(r)	care	oi	oil	zh	vision
ä	palm	oŏ	took		
e	end	ōō	pool	ə	**a** in about
ē	equal	ou	out		**e** in listen
i	it	u	up		**i** in pencil
ī	ice	û(r)	burn		**o** in melon
o	odd	yōō	use		**u** in circus

The Writing Process

WHEN WRITING, you can use a plan called the writing process to help you think of ideas and then write about them. These are the stages of the writing process. The writing process helps you move back and forth through stages of your writing.

PREWRITING

Identify your task, audience, and purpose. Then choose a topic. Gather and organize information about the topic.

DRAFTING

Put your ideas in writing. Don't worry about making mistakes. You can fix them later.

Prewriting Sometimes you might find it difficult to think of a topic. Ideas for topics can come from many places: something you already know or would like to know more about, something you've read, or something that has happened to you.

You can organize your ideas in several ways. You might use a list, an outline, a story map, a web, or a drawing.

Drafting When you put your ideas on paper, use your organizer to maintain the correct order. If you make a mistake, keep going. You can go back to it later.

Remember that when you finish each stage of the writing process, you can return to a previous stage or go on to the next stage. If you're not happy with what you've written, begin again.

Proofreading Once you have finished making changes, you are ready to fix your mistakes. Use editors' marks to fix mistakes and make changes. Use the Proofreading Checklist to help you.

Publishing Here are some ideas you can use.
- Read your story aloud.
- Turn it into a play or a Readers Theatre.
- Print it using a computer.
- Make an audiotape or a videotape.
- Illustrate your story, and show the pictures as your audience listens to you read.

RESPONDING AND REVISING

Reread your writing to see if it meets your purpose. Meet with a partner or group to discuss and revise it.

PROOFREADING

Correct any spelling, grammar, usage, mechanics, and capitalization errors.

PUBLISHING

Share your writing. Decide how you want to publish your work.

Responding and Revising When you read your own or someone else's writing, look for the following things: a good beginning and ending, clear words, and details about the topic.

When someone makes suggestions about your writing, you can decide whether or not to make those changes.

Proofreading Checklist

✓ Circle any words you are not sure you have spelled correctly. Then look them up in a dictionary, or ask someone who knows how to spell them.

✓ Look for words you have misspelled before. Add them to your Spelling Log.

✓ If you are unsure of how to spell a word, try saying the word slowly. Listen to every syllable. Have you written all the syllables?

✓ Make sure you have indented paragraphs.

✓ Check your capitalization and punctuation.

✓ Do you want to take out something or add something?

Spelling Strategies

Let us show you some of our favorite spelling strategies!

Here's a tip that helps me spell a word. I **say** the word. Then I **picture** the way it is spelled. Then I **write** it!

When I'm learning how to spell a word, the **Study Steps to Learn a Word** on pages 8 and 9 are a big help.

When I'm proofreading, I think of ways to spell the vowel sound in a word. Then I **try different spellings** until the word looks right.

When I don't know how to spell a word, I sometimes just take my best **guess!** Then I **check** it in a dictionary.

Sometimes I **read** the words **backward** when I'm proofreading. I start with the last word and end with the first word. It really helps me notice words I've misspelled! Then I proofread for meaning in the usual order.

Grade 5 • Harcourt Brace School Publishers

When I'm learning to spell a two-syllable word, I study the **pattern of letters** in each syllable. Then I look for **similar patterns** in other words.

When I'm writing a word that I know has a **homophone,** like *council* and *counsel,* I make sure I know **both meanings and spellings.** Then I use the word that makes sense.

When I proofread, I **keep track of my spelling errors.** I notice **the kinds of mistakes** I usually make, and this keeps me from misspelling the words so often.

I follow the **spelling rules** to change a word like *piano* to *pianist.* Then I check the **pronunciation key** in a dictionary to pronounce the **related word.**

When I'm writing a **compound word,** I think about how the **two smaller words** are spelled. Once I know this, I can check a dictionary to write the compound word in its correct form.

Drawing the **shape** of a word helps me remember how to spell it. This is the shape of the word flashlight.

When I'm proofreading, I check carefully to make sure I've included **"silent" letters**—like the *l* in *half* and the *s* in *island.*

Grade 5 • Harcourt Brace School Publishers

My Spelling Log

WHAT'S A SPELLING LOG? It's a special place where you can keep track of words that are important to you. Just look at what you'll find in your Spelling Log!

SPELLING ★ WORDS ★

Spelling Words to Study

This is just the place for you to list the words you need to study. There is a column for each unit of your spelling book.

WordShop ★ WORDS ★

Vocabulary WordShop Words

Every spelling lesson has a list of words on the Vocabulary WordShop page. List them where you think they belong on special pages for . . .

Language . . . page 186

Social Studies and Science . . . page 187

Art and Music . . . page 188

Your Own WORDS

My Own Word Collection

Be a word collector, and keep your collection here! Sort words you want to remember into fun categories you make up yourself!

Grade 5 • Harcourt Brace School Publishers

Spelling Words to Study

UNIT 1	UNIT 2
Lesson 1	Lesson 6
Lesson 2	Lesson 7
Lesson 3	Lesson 8
Lesson 4	Lesson 9
	Lesson 10

Grade 5 • Harcourt Brace School Publishers

Spelling Words to Study

UNIT 3	UNIT 4
Lesson 12	Lesson 18
	Lesson 19
Lesson 13	
	Lesson 20
Lesson 14	
	Lesson 21
Lesson 15	
	Lesson 22
Lesson 16	
	Lesson 23

Grade 5 • Harcourt Brace School Publishers

Spelling Words to Study

SPELLING ★ WORDS ★

UNIT 5	UNIT 6
Lesson 25	Lesson 31
Lesson 26	Lesson 32
Lesson 27	Lesson 33
Lesson 28	Lesson 34
Lesson 29	Lesson 35

Grade 5 • Harcourt Brace School Publishers

Language Words

These pages are for listing Vocabulary WordShop Words. Group words that you think go together in a category. The words may give you some ideas about ways to group them. Use ideas of your own, too!

Add a clue beside a word to help you remember it. The clue might be a picture, a sentence, a definition, or just a note.

Action Words

Friendly Words

Rhyming Words

Homophones

Fancy Words

Proper Nouns

Sound Words

Poetry Words

Soft Words

Grade 5 • Harcourt Brace School Publishers

Social Studies and Science Words

Put Social Studies and Science Words into groups on this page.

Animal and Plant Words

Transportation Words

Health Food Words

Weather Words

City Words

Desert Words

Map Words

Mountain Words

History Words

Jungle Words

Health Words

Grade 5 • Harcourt Brace School Publishers

Art and Music Words

This page is for Art and Music Words!

Favorite Song Words

Landscape Words

Musical Instrument Words

Jazz Words

Classical Words

Museum Words

Colorful Words

Names of Artists

Names of Musicians

Concert Words

Grade 5 • Harcourt Brace School Publishers

My Own Word Collection

When you read and listen, be on the lookout for words you want to remember.
Group them into categories any way you like, and write them on these pages.
Pretty soon you'll have a word collection of your very own!

Video Game Words

Noisy Words

Outdoor Words

Exciting Words!!!

Skateboard Words

My Own Word Collection

Save words you really like in My Own Word Collection.
Include words you have trouble pronouncing or spelling.

Slang

Scary Words

Sports Words

Cartoon Words

Computer Words

Grade 5 • Harcourt Brace School Publishers